Mall of America

For Duke,
You were a great
student to work with —
curious, ambitious and certainly
irreverent. I hope you find
some of those qualities here.
With affection,
Eric
12/28/99

Mall of America

Reflections of a Virtual Community

Eric Nelson

1998
Galde Press, Inc.
PO Box 460, Lakeville, Minnesota 55044–0460, U.S.A.

First Edition
First Printing, 1998

Library of Congress Cataloging-in-Publication Data
Nelson, Eric, 1942–
    Mall of America : reflections of a virtual community /
Eric Nelson.—1st ed.
        p.   cm.
    ISBN 1–880090–58–9 (trade pbk.)
    1. Mall of America (Bloomington, Minn.)
    2. Shopping malls—Social aspects—United States.
    3. United States—Social life and customs—1971–
I. Title.
HF5430.5.B58N45   1997
381'.1'0977657—dc21   97–45765
                                                          CIP

Galde Press, Inc.
PO Box 460
Lakeville, Minnesota 55044

For Riki and Benno

"We are planning to create a community."
—Donald Dayton, 1952,
        announcing the construction
        of the first enclosed mall
        in the United States at
        Southdale, Minnesota

Contents

Acknowledgements

I AM GRATEFUL FOR the timely and generous support provided by the Hustved family and St. Olaf College through the Hustved fellowship that released me from teaching in the spring of 1993. Thanks also to Carol Leach for her sharp editor's advice in an earlier stage of this project, to Sue Oiness for her indefatigable patience in retyping many revisions, and to Norm Watt for help in the final line editing. Thanks also to the many people who shared their stories with me. Last, but not least, thanks to my son Benno for pushing me to finally get this into print.

Preface

WHEN THE MALL OF AMERICA opened in August 1992, it was by no means clear that it would be a success (as my initial chapter, "Gala Opening," indicates). I decided at that time, however, to begin a book on the Mall and to explore its fortunes and evolving character. Given its dimensions and aspirations, it could very well be a mirror of contemporary America. Indeed, four years after its opening, it had become, according to a survey by the National Park Service, the most popular tourist destination in the U.S. The *New York Times* has reported that it draws more visits annually than Disney World, the Grand Canyon, and Graceland combined—forty million. Northwest, the Mall of America's "official airline," regularly brings in shopping junkets from Europe, Israel, Japan, Australia. Is it size alone that makes it such a magnet?

Or has the Mall of America established itself as an icon of U.S. culture? If it has, the causes are deeper than the megamall's prodigious public relations efforts. Malls are an inescapable feature of our common life. They seem as inevitable as the weather, so familiar we hardly think about them any more. As my subtitle suggests, I have attempted to think about them, that is to think about us, by using the megamall as a lens to magnify values in contemporary America. Each of the chapters explores a particular theme.

1. Gala Opening. Covers three days of the Mall's opening in 1992 and the divided opinion regarding its prospects.

2. It's a Wonderful Life. Traces the evolution of retail in the U.S. from general stores to suburban malls and looks at how these changes have influenced the character of community in the country. It ends with a focus on Bloomington, Minnesota, as a paradigmatic example of these historical changes.

3. Charlie Brown in the Field of Dreams. Examines American pop culture heroes as these are celebrated and exploited in the Mall: athletes, movie and comic book superheroes, the Peanuts characters. What do these reveal about our desires and fantasies?

4. Attitude Adjustment. Gender roles and changes in relations between the sexes as these are manifested in the Mall's shops, restaurants, nightclubs.

5. Cowboys and Indians. A look at the marketing of two mythologized themes in American history: the history of denim jeans and the synergistic connection between the reservation casinos and the Mall.

6. A Village School. The Leila Anderson Learning Center in the Mall. The focus is on a class of disadvantaged students in a work-study program of entrepreneurship.

7. Generation X and the Way the World Is. One year St. Olaf College bused its entering class up to the Mall as a way of introducing them to a liberal arts education. These students, in contrast to those of the preceding chapter, were affluent and white. How did they see the social and economic realities represented by the Mall?

8. Frankenstein, the Inner Child. Begins by exploring the Lego Imagination Center in the Mall and goes on to look at the evolution of Legos into more high-tech possibilities.

9. The Whirlwind. The first U.S. enclosed mall—Southdale—was built in Minnesota because of the state's forbidding weather. The chapter explores attitudes toward weather and nature generally, the control and marketing of these. The story behind the Rainforest Cafe.

10. The Underground Man. Not everyone dreams the standard American Dream. A skeptical perspective from a homeless person who worked at the Mall but remained indifferent to its seductions.

11. The Unknown God of the Mall. A final view of the Mall from a spiritual perspective.

Throughout, I have tried to avoid two extremes—puffing the Mall of America or giving it a predictable liberal bashing. I have sought rather to be playful and informative. The examples and anecdotes are taken from a period of five years. Most of the stores, restaurants, and nightclubs I allude to are still in the Mall, though some—for example, Tempus Expeditions, Dew Ann's Too, Gatlin Brothers Music City—have departed. When I spoke to Doreen Day at a Dakota pow-wow (chapter 5), she was Director of Indian Family Services in Minneapolis, a position she no longer holds. (Keeping this book up to date in all its details would entail rewriting it every week.) The Mall of America is like Heraclitus's river; it is always changing. But the French proverb applies: the more it changes, the more it stays the same.

Chapter One

Gala Opening

Monday, August 10, 1992

Normally, the opening of a mall is not one of those times when each of us must stand and be counted, but the Mall of America is not an ordinary mall. As the day of the gala opening drew nearer, it seemed that my fellow Minnesotans looked askance at me when I told them I had no strong opinion about whether this would be a happy event or an ominous turning of history. It's the biggest enclosed mall in the U.S., the second biggest in the world, and it was built on the site of the old Met Stadium in Bloomington, where the Twins and the Vikings played until they moved into the Metrodome downtown. When the teams and their fans left, Bloomington city officials invited down the three Ghermezian brothers, Iranians who had made a fortune selling Persian rugs and then gone on to assemble a billion-dollar mall in West Edmonton: eleven anchors and six hundred stores, a twenty-two-ride

1

amusement park, a life-size replica of the Santa Maria on a four-acre lake, four submarines, and a water park complete with a slide, bungee jumping, and a wave pool. The Ghermezians envisioned something even bolder in Bloomington.

Seven years later, the Bloomington mall opened, scaled down from the original fantasy. The hyper-aquarium was delayed a few years, the airport-to-mall monorail became a ten-minute shuttle-bus service. This new mall wasn't quite as big as that West Edmonton Ur-Mall, but it was still big enough to contain:

32 Boeing 747 aircraft
27 Lincoln Memorials
34 "normal" shopping malls
88 football fields

The floor space of this megamall, four point two million square feet, is about the same as in the Sears Tower in Chicago, the tallest building in the U.S. In July 1992, *U.S.A. Today* called it "the Mount Rushmore of retail" and asked, "Will people drive two thousand miles to walk its three miles of corridors?" Stories on the mall appeared throughout that summer in the *New York Times*, the *Philadelphia Inquirer*, the *Washington Post*, the *Chicago Tribune*, the *Los Angeles Times*...

Some of these stories were a bit condescending. "That America's Mall was built in Minnesota seems ironic to some," wrote a staff writer of the *L.A. Times*. "Home to dour Scandinavians with conservative life style and liberal politics, the state has always had an unextravagant sort of bent. When Norwest built a new 57-story headquarters in downtown Minneapolis during the 1980s, it consciously made the place 30 inches shorter than the city's tallest building rather than seem boastful or impolite." This particular stereotype has gotten quite a bit of air time in recent years in Garrison Keillor's folk epic, "The News from Lake Wobegon," where "all the women are strong and all the men are good looking and all the children are above average." Lake Wobegon is a small town, of course, but people from the coasts see Minnesota as a state of small towns, including Minneapolis-St. Paul, a Lake Wobegon with skyscrapers. We're one of the fly-over states.

Those of us who live in Minnesota prefer the term "heartland." Common sense is the great heartland virtue and a number of Minnesotans I talked to said it didn't make sense to open a megamall just as everyone was finally realizing that the eighties, that appalling decade of greed and extravagance, had burdened us with megadebt, high unemployment and shaky consumer confidence. Building a megamall now, these friends told me, is about as prudent as appointing Jay Gatsby to be the state's commissioner of finance.

A number of folks tried to bring the Mall project to a halt. A mayor of Bloomington who had been a strong supporter of the project got voted out of office and deep local skepticism had been vocal from start to finish. The Ghermezian brothers, with a negotiating style more Mideast than Midwest, were moved into the background and the Simon Brothers, Mel and Herb from Indianapolis, took charge. When they did, the Teachers' Insurance and Annuity Association of America agreed to invest the lion's share of the $625 million. TIAA is a conservative investor, as it should be with the futures of the nation's teachers, including mine. In 1992, I had $39,276.34 of the $58 billion of TIAA's assets, so I couldn't honestly claim that I had much of a personal stake. But if it is true that molecules of air once breathed by Jesus, by the Buddha, are still part of the weather and that some of these molecules could conceivably find their way into my lungs (and I have it on good authority that this is a very real possibility), then it isn't too far-fetched to say that I've put my two cents into the Mall of America. As in so many decisions about my future these days, I wasn't consulted and I was a wee bit uneasy. I had a stake in this extravagance and in a tiny way I was responsible for its coming into being. Maybe some sort of judgment was called for. Before making that judgment, though, I felt I should at least take a look at what I would judge. So I bought a pair of tickets for the gala opening.

As my wife Riki and I approached Bloomington, a big sign identified the lanes leading to the Mall of America and Killebrew Drive, the old access to Met Stadium, which provided a smooth entry up and around the Thing Itself, its red, white, and blue banner splashed overhead. We parked and were directed to one of the main entrances, where we were given bold designer shopping bags. The full-page ads for this Grand Opening Gala had said, "Tuxes and Tennies, Sequins and Sneakers," and right away I noticed that all men but me were wearing tuxes and high top tennis shoes. The ads also promised Ray Charles • Sandi Patti • the Gatlin Brothers • Peter Graves • Miss America • The Sounds of Blackness • Rupert's Orchestra • More than 250 Entertainers • Themed Buffets • Plus Special Surprises Throughout the Mall.

The first thing we ran into was one of the Special Surprises: Batman, Cat Woman, and the Batmobile, all courtesy of Time-Warner, which had a Warner Brothers Studio store in the Mall. (At this point I was willing to give it a capital letter.) Once we got to the Mall proper, we stepped into a benign pandemonium. All 250 entertainers seemed to be performing simultaneously in an opera by John Cage. A small group of Native Americans danced in circles, bizarrely and forlornly out of place, all of them minors except for two mothers. The children grinned sheepishly at each other: was this for real? Kitty-corner from them, a middle-aged group from New Ulm, Minnesota, did some Bohemian dances in native costumes. Farther down, a stage was mocked up as a California beach and two guitarists and a drummer were doing riffs on some song from the sixties I couldn't quite identify. The lead guitarist was in his fifties, dressed in a Hawaiian shirt, his hair pulled back in a ponytail. As we approached, a young woman gave us sunglasses with dayglo frames, and I noticed that the guys standing around, all of them in tuxes, were in their twenties, thirties, and forties. Some of them had ponytails too and they were wearing these dayglo sunglasses, listening respectfully, no chatter. The musicians finished their number and got a warm round of applause. They announced they were going to take a break and the small crowd dispersed. Riki went up to the lead guitarist and complimented him on his playing. She told him that our son was a lead guitarist in a rock band. He gave her one of his guitar picks and told us he was Dick Dale and that his group, the Deltones, did the music in all those beach party movies.

If Jay Gatsby had found his Daisy in the Midwest rather than in West Egg, his parties might have been something like this. The flow of champagne was endless and the themed buffets, to judge by the Minnesota and New Orleans Cajun tables, were loaded with tasty food. A number of female guests were also themed, though it was difficult to pin down just what these themes were. There was one woman in her late fifties, abundant bleached hair and mascara eyes, who had fine legs that she showed off with a very short leather skirt stretched taut over a prominent pot belly: Las Vegas bordello?

The men dressed less adventurously. There was a Ted Turner look-alike wearing an "I Love Hooters" T-shirt, a leggy blonde in a red leather miniskirt on his arm. But no one truly mysterious, no one in a pink suit with a checkered past, no one who might once have murdered a man, though with more than nine thousand guests in all this space I could easily have missed him.

At 9:00 we all gathered around the main stage for the official opening ceremonies. The master of these ceremonies was Peter Graves, the star of the old "Mission Impossible" television series (an unintended irony here?). He was a Minneapolis boy, he reminded us, who had married a St. Paul girl. A huge screen overhead gave those of us farther back a fuller image of Peter, but I couldn't hear him very well. An honor guard with representatives from past wars, including the Persian

Gulf conflict, marched out, and Sandi Patti, who sang the National Anthem at the ceremony celebrating the restoration of the Statue of Liberty, did the same for the Mall of America, not singing it so much as doing riffs on it as if it were a torch song. Apparently nobody but Republicans sings the National Anthem straight these days. As Patti sang we got close-ups of the honor guard on the overhead screen.

Graves came back and again I caught only scraps of words and phrases. "...There's a dream in our lives like a flame that keeps burning...who made the Mall of America possible we thank you for your hard work...people who have lived and breathed...mayor...chairman of the board...Miss Minnesota would still be a dream...the great...of Minnesota, the honorable Arne Carlson." As he spoke, Peter kept touching his glasses as if they were about to slide off his face. He gave the impression of a cerebral Johnny Carson. Governor Carlson spoke briefly and unintelligibly ("We've heard all this before" was the only phrase I caught). Neil Peterson, the current Mayor of Bloomington, spoke: "...Needless to say, it's an incredible honor and privilege...the city of Bloomington...imagination and everything...zoning...dream...a reality...and now.... We got the fight won, ha, ha, ha!" This last he fairly shouted at the top of his lungs.

Chief executive officers were introduced and were joined by Charles Schulz and someone in a Snoopy costume and representatives from Nordstrom, Bloomingdale's, Macy's, Sears: "...exemplify these qualities...the man who...." The Ghermezian brothers came on stage, the Simon brothers came on stage, and finally everyone was lined up. A red, white, and blue ribbon descended. There was a countdown and the ribbon was cut. Images of eagles, Miss Liberty, and the flag filled the big screen overhead. And then Ray Charles was led to the piano on stage. He sat down and started to sing "America the Beautiful." Slowly orchestral accompaniment was piped in and then we were all singing along with Ray. At least I think we were singing along, I mean it sounded like we were, though I wasn't making a sound and I didn't see any mouths around me moving; still, most of us had to be singing and boy did we sound good, almost as good as Ray himself, all of us serendipitously in sync, singing our hearts out. Then it was over and Ray Charles was led off, graciously receiving our thunderous applause, humbly acknowledging our tribute with body gestures that, in another context, might have been misconstrued as bowing and scraping. There was no mistaking that smile, though. That smile was a patented trademark. Like the Mall logo that promptly burst into dazzling sparklers. Fireworks and lasers shot upward and eagles and Miss Liberty and the flag reappeared on the overhead screen.

The Mall of America was officially open.

Riki and I figured it was time to try some of the rides in Camp Snoopy. The carousel had wonderful demonic animals: giant rabbits, a dragon horse with a spiked tail, a stallion with a cherub peeping out of its saddle, a rooster, a leaping cat with a fish in its mouth, a bear, a giraffe, an ostrich. Their bodies were charged with power, nostrils flared, eyes wild. When it was our turn to climb on, a woman at the gate told Riki she could not ride sidesaddle. I watched her mount a rabbit very carefully: no problem. I missed my first choice, the dragon horse, so I got on the leaping cat. When the creatures sprang to life, a handsome couple ahead of me leaned toward each other and sent electricity back and forth with strokes and kisses.

The Kite-Eating Tree swung us out and away, round and round. I looked back at Riki in her chair, her eyes lit with excitement, her hair flying away.

Just as we got to the Ripsaw roller coaster, the woman at the gate told us they were closing down the rides for the night, so we wandered back to the main stage for the fireworks scheduled for 10:30. When they went off, Riki turned to me and said, "Wow, are they real fireworks?" My first impulse was to treat this as a silly question, but it triggered questions of my own: Was that the real Ray Charles? Were we really singing along with him? Were those real Indians dancing in a circle? Did Dick Dale and the Deltones really do the music for all those beach movies in the sixties?

After the fireworks we drifted around, occasionally bumping into look-alikes: Elvis, John Wayne, Mae West, Ernestine, Indiana Jones. We watched the Swedish dancers from Mora, Minnesota, getting themselves photographed against fake Nordic scenery. The party was winding down.

Riki went to look for a rest room and I sat down on a bench and waited for her. No longer filled with crowds and noise, the Mall seemed...just another mall. There was no particular shape or beauty to it, much less a magnificence that would put Disney World in the shade. I felt like a producer's friend in a screening room as the lights come back on, and I had this sad feeling in my gut that this movie was going to be a flop. I didn't have much at stake personally, just a few retirement pennies, but I felt let down anyway. I wondered how the folks involved in this production ever imagined it would pull in crowds. I wondered if they could see now that it was just not going to make it. This must be how the actors, writers, and the director feel at the wrap of a failed epic.

Riki returned and we headed out to the parking ramp. Coming in were a man and woman carrying what looked like overnight bags. The woman was wearing a gold bowler hat and comically big eyelashes. She stopped to ask the attendant something and I wondered, are some people going to sleep here tonight? Is there a hotel hidden somewhere? As we passed them I noticed her expression was one of anxious puzzlement, and I overheard the attendant saying to her, "When you came in through Gate One, did you turn left?"

We found our car easily and got onto Cedar Avenue, the most scenic route home. We drove through endless prairie under a full moon and neither of us said much. I turned on the radio and we listened to the Nutcracker Suite, Tchaikovsky's fantasia on Christmas extravagance. My earlier misgivings about the Mall returned.

Experts outside the state were dubious. There were now 38,000 malls in America, 1,400 built the previous year. According to Steve Clayton, president of MAS Mass Marketing Inc. of Chicago, "The whole project flies in the face of this high stressed, need-focused consumer today.... Entertainment and retailing, it will not work. They are in direct conflict with one another. They couldn't have designed it worse in terms of creating a consumer nightmare." Would a local shopper drive out of her way and battle an amusement park mob just to buy a skirt? Based on surveys in more than forty markets, MAS found that consumers in 1990 spent an average of four hours a month in malls, compared with twelve hours in 1980. Mall shoppers, according to this survey, also made fewer mall visits—2.1 a month in 1990 versus 3.1 in 1980—and shopped at fewer stores when they were at the mall—3.5 in 1990 compared with 7.0 in 1980.

None of the stats looked promising. Since the mid-1980s, the average vacancy rate for malls had risen nearly twelve percent, and many of the remaining tenants were paying less rent because sales were down. Management Horizons chairman Daniel Sweeney, in a speech to the International Council of Shopping Centers that year, predicted, "The industry is in a long term secular decline." The Minneapolis-St. Paul area, in the view of a real estate analyst for Solomon Brothers in New York City, had more than enough retail already. To meet the projections of the mall's developers, observed Dick Guidera, a Twin Cities retail and real estate consultant, "Every space in the parking ramp"—and we're talking thirteen thousand spaces—"would have to be used four times every day with two point two people in each car."

Yeah, but. It seemed to me there were just too many variables to predict the outcome. That weekend I had taken my father to the Canterbury Downs racetrack, the only thing in Minnesota he is interested in seeing when he visits me. He is just a two-dollar player, but on Saturday he couldn't pick a winner no matter how he boxed his bets. The sixth race was a simulcast from Monmouth Park in New Jersey, a race with a $500,000 cup. According to the racing form, it was a two-horse race: Strike the Gold, winner of the Kentucky Derby, and Fly So Free. Fly So Free was the slight favorite for reasons I have since forgotten. All kinds of factors enter into handicapping, too many for it to be a science. Neither Strike the Gold nor Fly So Free won or even finished in the money at Monmouth Park that afternoon.

The economy these days is that kind of horse race. You might as well wager on next week's weather. I realize that economists use software programs as subtle and elaborate as those used by the folks who map storm patterns, and I assume the field of economics attracts more powerful minds than meteorology (has a weatherman ever won a Nobel Prize?), but I have more faith in Willard Scott than I do in the Fed or the President's Council of Economic Advisors or anybody's council of economic advisors. And while I didn't doubt the stats and the expert opinion, the future of the Mall of America was, I felt, a crap shoot. Like the future of the nation.

Tuesday, August 11, 1992

We drove north toward the Twin Cities again. It was a beautiful morning, sunny, temperature in the low seventies, too good a day to spend indoors, as my mother used to tell me. On the radio someone was interviewing Senator Robert Kastin of Wisconsin about a memo he and Jack Kemp and Newt Gingrich had sent to then-President Bush apropos the upcoming Republican convention. Bush was way down in the polls, and I gathered the point of this memo was to urge him to define clearly for the voters a conservative agenda for the next four years. When asked what words he wanted to hear in the President's acceptance speech, Kastin said that "opportunity," "the future," and "vision" were central, with tax incentives to encourage investment as the best practical way to bring about a full economic recovery. I flipped off the news and watched the cornfields flash by.

When we got to Bloomington, Riki dropped me off at the Mall for its opening day and drove on to work in her studio. The doors had been open only an hour, but already the place seemed filled with people. Almost immediately, I ran into University of Minnesota cheerleaders shouting and prancing and waving gold pom-poms. Morning light was pouring down through the skylights and, in contrast to the previous night, the stores were wide open and ready for business. A fife and drum group in Revolutionary War uniforms was stationed in front of Filene's Basement. Rupert's orchestra was setting up at Bloomingdale's. At Naturalizer, a shoes and purse store, a young man in a tux handed a long-stemmed rose to each woman who entered.

"Only at Bloomingdale's." I stood in front of a wall of television screens, watching them change colors—blink, blink, blink, red, blue, black, green, magenta, blink, blink, blink— and I started to feel a strange tingling in the aura around my body, the aura getting bigger, my body getting smaller, and then a voice outside of me said, "Isn't that neat!" and I was back in Bloomingdale's, just like the sheik in the Arabian Nights who lifted a wine cup to his lips and was transported to another land where he had many adventures and married and fathered children and grew old, and just as he closed his eyes in death he woke up and was back in his tent and the wine was still running from his cup. I noticed that all around me young women dressed in black were staring into the glazed eyes of other women and painting their faces, or were urging them to sniff small vials and speaking to them very distinctly. I thought, maybe this is not Arabian Nights, maybe it's "Star Trek" and we have fallen under the control of intergalactic Amazons who have mastered techniques of autosuggestion and are here to redeem or destroy our planet.

A young man wearing a Credit to Go pin came up to me and asked, "Are you enjoying Bloomingdale's?"

"Yes," I said, very casually.

"Can I help you?" he asked.

I listened to my voice, still very casual, say, "How do I get back to the Mall?"

He led me along a maze lined with young women dressed in black to a place that opened out onto noise and a crowd, though it was not a place I remembered having been in before.

"It's kind of complicated," he told me. "I haven't seen the Mall myself yet. I'm going on my lunch break." I turned and walked slowly toward the crowd. I knew I would never see him again.

The Mall has its own geography and maps that show you how it works. East Broadway is a wide corridor of marble and brilliant geometric patterns of black and silver and white neon: New York, New York, bright lights, big city. Along West Market there is a mellower California glitz. Tall green columns sheathed in brass and encircled with lamps rise to a barrel-vaulted ceiling, like the roof of a train station in an old imperial city; at every level bridges trimmed in red and brass cross at swooping angles. South Avenue is—what?— antebellum Georgia? Minoan Crete? North Garden is a street paved with warm tiles and landscaped with tall palms and deciduous trees, old-fashioned street lamps, a marble foun- tain, and tiered balconies festooned with hanging flower beds. Palm trees and orchids in the North? The colors looked pretty balmy to me, more Mediterranean than Minnesotan, but then Minnesota is what all these people had come here to escape.

The whole idea of compass points was pointless anyway. This mall is designed to send you in loopy, convoluted orbits. Its real geography is the space-time pretzel logic of contem- porary physics, where each shopper is never more than thirty seconds away from fashion apparel, never more than two minutes from a children's store, a sports shop, a high-tech gewgaw, a sugar buzz. The horizon shrinks to a moment...this moment and this moment and this moment...in a Möbius strip almost three miles long. Like Einstein's universe, the Mall is always curving back on itself, everywhere a center without a circumference, getting bigger at the speed of light but never bigger than a single moment. This moment.

A fashion shop had a mannequin with long, frizzy black hair dressed in sheer flowery pants and a sheer flowery swing top, and the young saleswoman next to it was wearing the same outfit and had the same body, the same hair, the same face. In the window of Dejaiz, two young men danced wildly to pure silence. One looked Hispanic, the other was African- American; they both wore black caps with "Boy" blazoned across the front. Ten feet farther on I suddenly heard the beat behind their jive. Riki's question from last night came back to me. Is this for real? A critic of malls has described them as television you can walk around in. Moving through this mall was like channel surfing on super cable. I was on the edge of mild vertigo.

In the thirties, Walter Benjamin, a Jew adrift in Nazi Germany trying to make sense of history, realized that Hitler's Reich was not the only kingdom rooted in magic. To flee Berlin and fly to Paris was to exchange one collective madness for another, the Nazi will to power for a capitalist fairyland of inexhaustible desire, a fantasy that flowered in the shopping arcades of the nineteenth century. After the Napoleonic wars, the Palais Royal with its fashionable shops and restaurants, its dazzling entertainments under a circular roofed amphitheater, became a magnet for foreign visitors, famous throughout the continent. According to an illustrated guide to Paris of the time, "an arcade of this kind is a city, a world in miniature." Not surprisingly, arcades appeared in other countries and a typology took shape: independent shops were organized in symmetrical tiers in a public space on private property, protected from weather and traffic. These skylit and gaslit enclosures, created by entrepreneurs and speculators to market the ever-increasing luxury goods generated by high capitalism, offered customers not only merchandise but an "experience." A new form of recreation became the rage in Europe: strolling through the arcade, cruising, hanging out. The point wasn't to buy something, but to be drenched in a downpour of sensory overload. Endless commodities and entertainments do not gratify wishes but multiply them, and as anyone who has fallen in love knows, unsatisfied desire can be sweetly intoxicating.

To enter the arcades, Benjamin felt, was to enter an altered state where all the senses are heightened and all sensations are resonant, like symbols in a dream, but without the meaning or depth of a dream from which one might awaken. This was a dream of the social collective, Benjamin wrote. "Just as the sleeping person (here like someone insane) sets out on the macrocosmic journey through his body, and just as the sounds and sensations of his own insides…generate hallucinations or dream images, so it is too with the dreaming collective, which in the arcades sinks into its own innards."

Benjamin wasn't the only one who felt this way. About the same time, Franz Hessel reported similar feelings about his experience in Berlin's Kaisergalerie. "I cannot enter it without a damp chill coming over me, without the fear that I might never find the exit." Germany was a crazy place at this time, no question, but this particular craziness came out of the war stronger than ever and emigrated to America.

In the sixties, also a crazy time, Raquel Welch climbed into a submarine with a team of scientists and they were shrunk to the size of a microbe so they could travel through the human body in *Fantastic Voyage*. The movie simulated anatomical systems in Cinemascope and with Oscar-winning special effects, but oddly the brain, the goal of the mission, was disappointingly drab. It was literally gray matter. The cerebral cortex should have looked (on screen) like the Mall of America: an uncensored fantasia of pop culture and archaic appetite, every axon and dendrite glowing with neon intensity, dreaming Gatsby's dream, the orgiastic future that year by year recedes before us. In this subliminal mirage, the categories of real and unreal no longer apply. At Fabulous Fakes, the jewelry is fake, sure, but still fabulous, with a "lifetime guarantee." It's pointless to ask if, over there next to the Good Humor truck, that really is a white rabbit wearing a black bow tie and a moneychanger. All things are images in the dreaming collective; all things are possible.

For the first time I realized that this place was not just another mall as I had thought the night before. Now all the stores were buzzing with thousands and thousands of happy campers; Paul Bunyan's Log Chute, the Ripsaw roller coaster, and the Screaming Yellow Eagle had settled into a vaster landscape of chrome, color, and light. It was the difference between sitting in a screening room and sitting in a theater with real folks who have come for a good time. The Mall felt like a hit, a Jules Verne epic turned into virtual reality. Of course, it still might wind up in the red. The other day I had heard on the radio that Time-Warner calculated that *Batman,* one of the biggest moneymakers of all time, a cornucopia of merchandise and tie-ins, would never turn a profit. But profit isn't always the point.

Back in the Middle Ages, when they made cathedrals rather than movies, they didn't weigh the cost of their aspirations. Maybe the Mall should be seen as an expression of spirit rather than street smarts, more like the moonshot than like Trump Towers, a Chartres with its flying buttresses inside, binding all this mass and energy, crowds pulled down sweeping vectors the way gravity holds the galaxies, turning and turning in a widening gyre. Not anarchy loosed upon the world, but postmodern Gothic. "It is that strange disquietude of the Gothic Spirit," John Ruskin remarked, "that is its greatness; that restlessness of the dreaming mind, that wanders hither and thither among the niches, and flickers feverishly around the pinnacles, and frets and fades in labyrinthine knots and shadows along wall and roof, and yet is not satisfied, nor shall be satisfied."

Vertigo again. I needed to get something to eat. It was 2:30 now and I figured the lines at the fast food places in the Food Courts would be shorter. All I wanted really was a newspaper, a cup of coffee, and a place to sit. I checked my Mall map under the category "Books, Stationery," and saw that there were five places that sold reading material: B. Dalton (N 184), News Emporium (N 320), News, Etc. (W 153), P. G. Pages (S 140), and Street Corner News (E 119). All but one of these were on level one, but I decided that since I was already on level three I'd try the News Emporium.

The N 300-N 320 shops were on North Garden close to Nordstrom, three places up from Park Place and Boardwalk (joke). I was on East Broadway near Bloomingdale's. I turned left at Sears and headed down North Garden. I was now where N300-N320 should have been, but I was damned if I could see a News Emporium. There was Nordstrom right where it was supposed to be, but no News Emporium. None of this seemed familiar anyway, but it had to be up here somewhere.

Down West Market toward Macy's...left at Macy's... South Avenue. I was beginning to feel I was wandering

through a labyrinth without a string. Nothing...nothing...
nothing....It's hard to concentrate when at every step your
eye is pulled in all directions....I was back at Bloomingdale's.
Okay, one more time, slowly...3:45 and still no News Emporium. I rechecked "Books, Stationery." N 320. Was I on the
right level? I went to the balcony, leaned over and
counted...good grief. Lost in Wonderland.

"Would you tell me, please, which way I ought to go
from here?" I asked the Cheshire cat on my right.

"That depends a good deal on where you want to get
to," said the cat.

"I don't much care where—" I replied.

"Then it doesn't matter which way you go."

"—so long as I get somewhere."

"Oh, you're sure to do that," the cat assured me, "if only
you walk long enough."

I was on level one now, where there should have been
three places to buy a newspaper, and once again I was going
in a circle. I realized that drifting through this mall was one
thing, conducting a purposeful search quite another. Right,
forget the paper. Coffee and a place to sit. I'd already passed
several coffee shops, but I doubted that I'd ever find them
again. There: a Cinnabon shop with coffee. Not my first
choice, but any port in a storm. I got in line and when I
reached the counter I was so addled I ordered coffee *and* a
Cinnabon, a cardiac arrest dripping with sugar and choles-
terol. The coffee was very hot. I could barely hold it, and
now I noticed there was no place to sit down, not even on
the floor; all the space next to walls in the immediate area

was occupied, but I was going to drop the scalding cup any second, so I sat down in the middle of the corridor in front of a potted plant. I began eating my Cinnabon...eating...eating...another impossible quest. I chucked it into the trash can next to me. I sipped my coffee and watched the traffic at floor level and thought of those cowboy movies I loved as a boy where the second unit filmed these terrific stampede sequences by digging a hole and climbing in and shooting the cattle as they leaped over.

I had to get off my butt if I wanted to make it to my rendezvous with Riki, in front of Macy's, by 4:30. I got there just as she did, and we decided to go to one of the nightclubs on the Upper East Side for a happy hour drink. En route, Riki stopped at Macy's and bought a pair of socks printed with a Roy Lichtenstein cartoon. Up on level four there was God's plenty to choose from: America's Original Sports Bar, Hooters, Fat Tuesday, Gatlin Brothers Music City, Knuckleheads, Little Ditty's, Puzzles, Gators... We decided on Fat Tuesday, which has a New Orleans-Cajun theme. A waitress encouraged us to go to the bar and sample a few of their more than thirty-two frozen drinks. All these drinks were mixed and ready behind glass portholes that displayed their colors, bright pastels ranging from pale pink to organdy and deep rose, like a soda fountain. We selected two to taste in small paper cups, and the youthful bartender, who clearly thought our choices were too cautious, added two more of his own: 190 Octane, made with vodka, grain alcohol, and orange, and Purple Passion, concocted from 151-proof rum, bourbon, grape, and "other juices." The possibilities seemed endless. Headbutt, with three kinds of rum and fruit juice; Candy Bar, "like a Fudgsicle, crème de cocoa"; or better yet, the Tootsie Roll Pop, which mixes 190 Octane and Candy Bar. A lot of these drinks were mix-and-match and had names like Killer Bees, Redneck Lemonade, and Triple Bypass. We ordered just one, Bahama Mama, one of the more modest offerings, in a medium portion with two straws.

We took our drink to a table next to a broad window that looked out on Camp Snoopy. We sipped slowly and watched. The Screaming Yellow Eagle swept its riders up to our eye level, and we gazed into the riders' faces for a moment before they plunged to earth. It was five o'clock and the crowds had thinned considerably. This would have been a good time to try some of the more popular rides, but we were not up for a Bahama Mama-Ripsaw roller coaster combo. We saved that adventure for another day.

By six, we were on the road.

Wednesday, August 12, 1992

My father and I sat in the Ole Store in Northfield and waited for the waitress to come and take our breakfast orders. He had flown in Friday for a brief visit and would be leaving that afternoon. Before going home, he wanted to have the Ole Store specialty, an Ole Roll. To the innocent eye, an Ole Roll is indistinguishable from a caramel nut roll you might buy anywhere, but as any Ole Store patron will tell you, Ole Rolls are to those pale substitutes what Coke is to the competition. We had bought a paper and divided it up, the sports section to him, the rest to me. The waitress came, took our orders, and poured us coffee, and my father asked, "Did you see that movie to the end?"

"Yeah, it was pretty good."

My father shook his head and said, "That guy was nuts," repeating the judgment he had made the night before when he got up and went to bed. We had been watching *Bugsy,* which I had rented at the local video store because I was too exhausted after my day at the Mall to do anything else. Warren Beatty gave Bugsy Siegel's decline and fall a romantic spin, a sort of update on the Great Gatsby story. Early in the film, there is a scene where Bugsy forces a man to his knees and orders him to bark and oink. My father had stood up and remarked, "He's nuts," and said good night. There aren't too many movies he's willing to sit through.

I liked the movie. It certainly isn't your typical gangster picture. The tone is an odd mix of whimsy and brutality. Siegel goes to Southern California and gets involved in the movie community; he even has a screen test made of himself. He has some fairly crazy ideas: he will go to Italy and assassinate Mussolini and then he will build a gambling hotel-casino in the middle of the Nevada desert. Mussolini dies before Bugsy can get to Italy, but he does convince the Mob to bankroll his casino idea. The Flamingo won't be your run-of-the-mill operation. There will be a stage for shows and guest performances by celebrities, a swimming pool, air-conditioning throughout, so the investment will be considerable: one million dollars. Actually, it ends up costing six million, and when no one shows up for the gala opening on Christmas, Bugsy's partners blow his head off. Bugsy himself keeps faith with his vision to the end, and at the conclusion of the picture we are told that the Flamingo grossed $100 billion by 1991. To say nothing of the entire city of Las Vegas that mushroomed around it.

The movie presents Bugsy as a bohemian mobster, a creator willing to risk everything to realize his vision (his word for it). He's a Van Gogh who cuts off other people's ears, and as with Van Gogh we know he's great because of the astronomical appreciation of his initial investment. It's always easy to spot a fruitful innovation in hindsight. As you watch *Bugsy,* you laugh at the plan to assassinate Mussolini (what a whacko notion!) and you savor the irony of his preposterous hopes for the Flamingo. A pleasure palace hundreds of arid miles from population centers is a brilliant idea ahead of its time. But what if history had turned out differently, what if Bugsy had sacrificed himself in a successful assassination of Il Duce that altered the course of World War II and so was not able to pursue his Flamingo inspiration? We would be chuckling at his casino pipe dream (what a whacko notion!) and we'd get a lump in our throats anticipating his mission to Italy. In the movie's conclusion, Bugsy says good-bye to Virginia Hill, his Hollywood mistress, before he climbs into a prop plane to fly to his death. The scene is shot in a way reminiscent of the ending of *Casablanca.*

Imagine Bugsy saying to his mistress, "I've got a job to do and where I'm going you can't follow, what I've got to do you can't be a part of. Virginia, I'm no good at being noble, but it doesn't take much to see that the problems of two little people don't amount to a hill of beans in this crazy world.

Someday you'll understand that. Now now. Here's looking at you, kid."

On the other hand, let's just go with the actual turn of events. Bugsy didn't kill Mussolini; Las Vegas became a boomtown. The Flamingo grossed one hundred billion by 1991. Bugsy was right after all. Or was he? By a different measure, the Flamingo could be seen as a terrible idea. I had read a story in the Minneapolis *Star Tribune* a few days earlier that reported Nevada to be one of the sickest states in the Union, ranking poorly in everything from the incidence of lung and liver disease to the high rate of cancer deaths and new AIDS cases. Nevadans are more likely than other Americans to die in the work place or in automobile accidents, and the suicide rate is twice the national average. The article attributed this sad state of affairs to the indulgent, excessive lifestyle spawned by Nevada's gaming industry. What if *Bugsy* ended with these statistics rather than the Flamingo's revenues?

Nevada's neighbor, Utah, by the way, ranked as the third healthiest state in the U.S., a difference attributed to the influence of the Mormon Church, which discourages alcohol and tobacco use. The Church of Jesus Christ of Latter-day Saints is another one of those crackpot inspirations that wound up changing history. Brigham Young's vision, if anything, seemed more far-fetched and dangerous in the middle of the nineteenth century than Bugsy's did in the 1940s. Both men repeated the journey of Moses, leading a small band of social outcasts (true believers in the case of Young, skeptical killers in the case of Siegel) through the desert to a Promised Land.

Warren Beatty, apparently, was one of those who believed in Bugsy, or at least believed in Bugsy the artist. Bugsy's story, after all, was his story: a man with a fantasy must persuade other men, hard-headed money men, to invest millions in the realization of his fantasy, and then pour in millions more when the budget spirals out of sight, and then persuade millions of ordinary people all over the world to justify this extravagance by lining up to pay the price of admission. Bugsy's battle to build the Flamingo isn't much different from the way movies get made. Christopher Columbus may or may not have "discovered" America, depending on your point of view. There can be no disputing, however, that he gave us something else at least as important as a New World. He gave us our definition of success: selling an illusion. It's called the American Dream.

I turned back to the morning paper. Its headline read, "Heeding the Mall's Call." One hundred and fifty thousand people, I learned, showed up for the opening yesterday. There was no gridlock near the Mall, as had been feared, but all thirteen thousand parking places in the two ramps were filled by noon and the overflow had to be sent to off-site parking. The four anchor stores apparently did a brisk business, though smaller specialty shops did less well. Twenty thousand rides were taken in the first four hours at Camp Snoopy. By noon, seventy wheel chairs had been checked out; by 5:00 P.M. five hundred strollers had been requested. Seven hundred fifty children made hand prints in the freshly poured cement outside Macy's, and fifteen children got lost and were reunited with their families. At 9:05 A.M., Victoria's Secret recorded its first sale, a pair of thirty-dollar blue/paisley silk men's boxer shorts, the kind Jay Gatsby might have slipped into after he had waved away the last of his drunken guests.

So we beat on, boats against the current, borne back ceaselessly into the past.

Chapter Two

It's a Wonderful Life

AT THE BEGINNING OF THE NINETEENTH CENTURY, there were only a dozen cities in the United States with a population of five thousand or more that could support shops specializing in just one kind of merchandise—stationery, boots and shoes, china and glass, hardware. If you did not live in one of these cities, as the vast majority of Americans did not, you went to one store, a general store, with all your needs. The general store goes back to medieval Europe, where, in cities like London and Paris, mercers, haberdashers, and drapers were permitted to trade in all kinds of merchandise, in contrast to other shopkeepers who, restricted by guild regulations, sold only the articles they manufactured. In the New World, the general store was reinvented, a hybrid of necessity and Yankee ingenuity. The place was unpainted and not very large, perhaps twenty by thirty feet; the doors were narrow and the front windows small-paned. The floors were dark with the stains of filth, the ceiling overhead blackened from smoke. More often than not you paid with labor or in kind instead of with cash, exchanging butter and rag coverlets for a halter and chewing tobacco, or helped to raise a barn or mowed a hay field to clear a debt.

The merchant had to know the market values of everything from veal to wood ashes. If he accepted fresh eggs in barter, it was up to him to determine their degree of freshness. Eggs left in the sun might hatch into chicks an hour or two after the farmer's wife had gone on with her bit of gingham. For their part, customers had to have a sharp eye and tongue to test for sand in sugar, water in rum, dust in pepper, chicory in coffee, lard in butter. The frontier form of the Golden Rule ran, "If you don't look after yourself, no one else will." Naturally each family depended on its own resourcefulness wherever possible, mending, fixing, patching, improvising, making do. But even the most stoical and self-sufficient needed some bright thread now and again, or a harmonica, or a bit of licorice. All things considered, the merchant had the upper hand. He knew what the market would bear; he had daily opportunities to hone his bargaining skills. Country folk were inclined to take a skeptical, even mistrustful view of merchants. A storekeeper might know the worth of a sheepskin to the penny, but he could not smell a shift in the weather or cure a calf of the croup. He was often soft, untested in the serious challenges of survival, not tough or savvy enough in the ways that mattered out in the wilderness.

Like him or not, you needed your local merchant. He served the community as middle man, issuer of credit, banker, supplier of necessities and some luxuries, shipper of farm crops and local manufactures. Just as important for men, he had a warm fire away from home. "Only the tavern and the barber shop have ever offered serious competition to the old general store as a place of male refuge," Gerald Carson observes in *The Old Country Store,* "where a man could spit, scratch, and make up stories which everyone enjoyed and nobody believed, in an atmosphere of gemütlichkeit…. Since the storekeeper kept the post office too, the newspapers were generally well read in the store before they reached the hands of the subscribers."

Starting around the turn of this century, general stores were driven into extinction by more robust species of retail. Yet the idea that informed the general store persisted and evolved through these new forms of merchandising. Homology is a biological term that refers to a form that persists in a variety of creatures. The human hand, for example, and the mole's forelimb, the horse's leg, the porpoise's paddle, and the bat's wing are all constructed on the same pattern, with similar bones in the same relative positions. Scale varies but the pattern remains. "The cat-sized hyrax," Gregory Bateson once remarked, "is close to being a hippopotamus, and the lion is very close to being a pussycat." Features and functions that weather the storms of natural selection reproduce themselves in ever more refined adaptations.

In the second half of the nineteenth century a larger and more glamorous variant of our native homology—a diversity of merchandise under one roof—sprang up in the cen-

ters of major cities: A. T. Stewart's; Lord & Taylor; Arnold
Constable; R. H. Macy's in New York; John Wannamaker in
Philadelphia; Jordan Marsh in Boston; Field, Leiter & Co. (later
Marshall Field & Co.) in Chicago. They sold, as the general
store had, clothing for adults and children, small household
wares, dry goods, and home furnishings, but in much greater
volume and on a far grander scale. Merchandise had to be organized into departments, hence the term department store. Pride
of place as the first department store has traditionally been
awarded to Bon Marché of Paris, with W. Hitchcock and
Co. of London also a strong contender. Both evolved gradu-
ally from modest dry goods stores, as did Macy's of New York.

The department store offered more than just expanded
retail, however. It was an environment in which consumption became a dazzling entertainment, meant to appeal to
women who had become the primary shoppers. Macy's staff
contained a large proportion of women and girls, and one of
them, Margaret Getchell, hired in 1861 as a cashier, eventually became store superintendent. In his *History of Macy's
of New York, 1858-1919,* Ralph Hower speculates that
she was "the first of her sex to attain an executive position
in American business."

"Her importance in the history of the store," Hower
notes, "transcends routine supervision. She apparently influenced Macy's policy on many occasions, and...she initiated
several new lines of merchandise in the store." She encouraged management to expand their inventory of fancy goods
to include clocks, silver-plated ware, and Gorham's solid silver,
and to add a new department devoted to a wide selection

of house furnishings: kitchen utensils, wooden ware, baskets, bird cages, brushes, dusters, baby carriages, and a larger stock of plated ware.

Gone were the cramped dimensions and smoke-blackened ceilings of the frontier. Before the era of electric lighting, elevators, and escalators, there was in all the large stores a central rotunda flooded with natural light from a glass dome, and a grand stairway that rose to the encircling galleries overhead. Slender iron columns allowed shoppers to survey vistas of seductively presented merchandise, all of which was arranged for maximum convenience. The main floor offered small cash-and-carry commodities, an arena for impulse buying: notions, haberdashery, gloves, stockings, cosmetics, candies, stationery, books, local souvenirs. The men's department was also on the ground floor to accommodate those who had no interest in recreational shopping and could make their purchases quickly and efficiently. Fashion and children's clothing were on the next one or two floors, and the most serious purchases, such as furniture and carpets, were displayed on still higher levels. A subtle and elaborate calculus organized the arrangement of everything, and everything was made to seem affordable. A fixed-price, one-price policy; free delivery; freedom to exchange or return goods; charge accounts; name brands: these innovations "democratized luxury." Satisfaction guaranteed or your money back.

The wares and the money to buy them had been generated by the economic boom that had followed the Civil War. Industrial capacity mushroomed and a prosperous middle class was eager for more than just the necessities of life. In their purchases, they sought a "lifestyle." This new self-conception, one defined and expressed through possessions, was later mythologized in the figure of Jay Gatsby. Gatsby's house, his car, his shirts, the books in his library are for him a medium of self-creation, his way of becoming real by making an impression on others.

The big department stores prospered by encouraging and catering to this new understanding of consumption. They marketed and made respectable Gatsby pretensions. From the very start Rowland Macy was an aggressive, savvy advertiser. In 1887 he offered "Goods suitable for the millionaire at prices in the reach of millions." One year later the first successful large-scale electric traction system of transportation was launched in Richmond, Virginia, and soon trolleys were bringing even more eager customers to the doors of the great emporiums. By the turn of the century these customers were pampered with electric lights, hydraulic elevators, and an early form of air conditioning. And when, decades later, the middle class fled the congestion of cities to the quieter suburbs, the department stores followed. They were still marketing lifestyles.

Conspicuous consumption might be just the thing for city dwellers, but what were country mice to do? Until this century most of the population was rural. It took someone who grew up in the sticks to figure out a way to bring industry's cornucopia of merchandise to these broadly scattered homesteads and towns. In 1887, the year Rowland Macy lured urban shoppers with goods suitable for a millionaire at prices within the reach of millions, a fellow from Minnesota went to Chicago and teamed up with Alvah Curtis Roebuck to launch a mail order business aimed at folks on the prairie. Richard Sears had been a railroad station agent at North Redwood, a village of three houses. He knew how isolated people could become out on the Great Plains; the railroad was their lifeline. As a station agent he was able to secure special freight rates, and he turned a healthy profit selling wood, coal, and lumber to farmers and Indians at low cost. Then he tried his hand at marketing a luxury item, watches, buying them wholesale from Chicago and selling them through other agents along the line. He didn't stay in North Redwood very long.

In the 1890s Sears, Roebuck and Company offered to everyone within reach of the U.S. Postal Service an inventory that embraced sofas and sewing machines, trombones and trusses. People didn't need to come to a store to browse; they could browse through the company catalog. The first edition, published in 1893, had 196 pages and cost a nickel. By 1894 it had 500 pages, and in 1903 Sears had its own press with four-color printing. Out in the countryside it was known as the Homestead Bible.

"In rural schoolhouses," historian Daniel Boorstin reports, "children were drilled in reading and spelling from the catalogue. They practiced arithmetic by filling out orders and adding up items. They tried their hand at drawing by copying the catalogue models, and acquired geography by studying the postal-zone maps."

The catalog wasn't the only reason Sears did a land office business in those years. Under the leadership of Postmaster General and department store tycoon John Wannamaker, the federal government instituted Rural Free Delivery in 1913, a service that made Sears products quite affordable. Parcel post and the mail order store marked the demise of the local general store and of thousands of tiny villages as well. In parcel post's first year, Sears Roebuck and Company received five times the number of orders it had in 1912. The trolleys brought customers to commodities in the cities; the trains now brought merchandise to the farmers. The arrival of each purchase from Sears was like a little Christmas. Farmers thought of John Sears not as a faraway CEO but as a local merchant, and when they sent in their orders they included in their letters personal news—a new birth, a marriage, an extension of the homestead.

Farm families, however, were brought into touch with a much wider community. Bringing newspapers and magazines as well as merchandise, parcel post was an information highway before the advent of fiber optics. The young were better able to compare life on the land with life in a city, a life of work versus a life of style. More and more of them packed their bags, as Richard Sears had done, and headed off to the main chance—Omaha, Kansas City, Minneapolis, or, most dazzling of all, Chicago. In 1860, Chicago had 109,260 inhabitants; by 1910 the number had risen to more than two million and it was the second largest city in the nation. Not as big as New York, but with more hustle, more energy. In Chicago only the sky was the limit.

I once stood on the top floor of Chicago's Sears Tower, the tallest building in the U.S., set in the most stunning skyline in the country, especially dramatic when you drive into it from the North Shore. In the elevator that took me to the top (110 stories in seventy seconds, as I recall), a disembodied voice said that on a clear day you can see five states. I went up at night, so I didn't see five states but I did see the town spread out below in glowing constellations. I looked down on the other not-quite-so-tall skyscrapers arrayed about me, a gigantic Stonehenge lit up like a Christmas tree. I thought of God gazing at the galaxies and supergalaxies, zonked on their glory. Seen from above, Chicago's hustle and politics were resolved into a brilliant pattern that seemed to make sense. From the top of the Sears Tower, the city is a serene place at night; no hookers or turf wars, just darkness and electric configurations.

Chicago is proud of its skyscrapers. The first was built in 1889–91, the Second Leiter Building at State and Van Buren, and the rest sprang up like beanstalks far into the sky. They were pragmatic commercial buildings in which form followed function. As corporations expanded in the last decades of the nineteenth century, taking control of all aspects of production and distribution, their administration also grew in scope and complexity. Chicago was the prototype of a new city. The factories, requiring greater horizontal space, were pushed out to industrial parks in the suburbs, while management was shifted to the city center, close to financial services, and housed in buildings that moved upward rather than outward. Many a Jack sold his cow and started to climb his beanstalk in search of his fortune. In 1870 only one out of five Americans lived in a city with a population of eight thousand or more. By 1910 almost half the nation lived in cities. At the turn of the century, approximately a third of the country's manufacturing assets were consolidated into 318 giant companies.

Larger-than-life proportions, however, are not always an advantage, as Jack discovered up in the clouds. What was innovative in the 1890s was archaic in the 1990s. Too cumbersome, too expensive, and too inflexible for the post-modern marketplace. The new thinking favors "horizontal structure" and "accordion management." The kind of retail pioneered by Richard Sears is now transacted more cheaply and efficiently over television. The Sears catalog (1,556 pages in the last and final edition) is a Smithsonian artifact in an age of twenty-four-hour home shopping cable channels, where a host displays merchandise and interviews celebrities and designers. Talk about low overhead: a producer, a director, two engineers in the control room, a group of product coordinators, and a handful of robotic cameras. The QVC Network ("Quality, Value, Convenience") reaches a potential forty-five million homes. Telephone agents record each transaction (average call, two minutes) in an IBM mainframe computer and the order is flashed to one of three shipping sites, which fill an average of a hundred thousand orders a day.

Unable to compete effectively as a lumbering behemoth, Sears downsized, closing its smaller stores in smaller towns, surrendering the rural and downscale business on which the company was built. A lot of those towns have been downsizing themselves for much of the century, though it's hard to see how they can get much smaller. On the centenary of Mr. Sears's auspicious partnership with Mr. Roebuck, deaths were outnumbering births in 993 U.S. counties, ninety-five percent of them rural.

Corporate retail, however, has not yet abandoned rural America. Wal-Mart, which has supplanted Sears as America's most successful retail company, is yet another mutation of the old general store. In the 1870s the owner of a small dry goods store in Watertown, New York, decided to set up a "five-cent counter." He invested a hundred dollars in sundry items that could be sold for profit at a nickel—buttonhooks, watch keys, baby bibs, washbasins, soap, harmonicas, whatever. He instructed his assistant to arrange them attractively on a table with the price displayed prominently. When the assistant left that dry goods store in Watertown he took the concept with him. He bought in volume and he sold cheap. By 1895 F. W. Woolworth was operating twenty-eight "Five and Ten Cent Stores." By 1900 he had fifty-nine. Each store was small, yet the number of stores in the chain enabled Woolworth to harvest economies of scale.

He paid low wages and lived quite happily with a high employee turnover. The merchandise, after all, was so inexpensive it sold itself. "We must have cheap help," he wrote his manager in 1892, "or we cannot sell cheap goods. When a clerk gets so good she can get better wages elsewhere, let her go—for it does not require skilled and experienced salesladies to sell our goods...one thing is certain: we cannot afford to pay good wages and sell as we do now, and our clerks ought to know it."

Woolworth used display windows and bold red colors to pull customers into his stores, and once in they could, he maintained, "go entirely through them without once being pressed to buy anything." The entire inventory was a bargain, without the hassle of bargaining. Small change, but small change adds up. In 1913 it was Woolworth who owned the tallest skyscraper in the world.

Before long others gave their own spin to the economy store. The Piggly Wiggly grocery chain, like Woolworth's, instituted self-service, but added a new wrinkle: a floor plan of aisles that drew customers through all the merchandise on their way to the checkout counter. Seductive packaging and brand names invited more and more impulse buying. Charles Walgreen grafted the general store onto the pharmacy, added a lunch counter and soda fountain, and invented the modern drug store. There were five hundred of them in two hundred cities by the time he died in 1938.

When Sam Walton started out with his first Ben Franklin franchise in Newport, Arkansas, back in the fifties, he was just twenty-seven years old, but he was a go-getter. He went beyond the franchise book in buying cheaper and selling cheaper. Like old Woolworth, he knew if he could just get folks into his store the goods would sell themselves. One store, however, wasn't enough for Sam. He had "an itch to do business," as he put it in *Made in America,* so he "started repeating what worked, stamping out stores cookie-cutter style," saturating whole states with Wal-Marts.

In the early years Sam favored small communities, and that posed a problem for local merchants. Yet nothing roused Sam's ire like the accusation that he was out to crush the little guy.

"Of all the notions that I've heard about Wal-Mart, none has ever baffled me more than this idea that we are somehow the enemy of small-town America." It all depends, Sam figured, on what your idea of a small town is. Though he became the richest man in America, with a $50-billion retail business, Sam Walton always considered himself a small-town merchant.

"I can tell you that nobody has more love for the heyday of the small town retailing era than I do." In 1991 his company sold enough men's and women's underwear and socks "to put a pair on every person in America, with some to spare." The secret of that success, Sam claimed, was a paradox: "The bigger Wal-Mart gets, the more essential it is that we think small. Because that's exactly how we have become a huge corporation."

This conflict between corporate and local retail is a lot older than Wal-Mart. The Speaker of the Indiana House of Representatives complained in a letter to his constituents in the late 1920s, "The chain stores are undermining the foundation of our entire local happiness and prosperity. They have destroyed our home markets and merchants, paying a minimum to our local enterprises, sapping the life-blood of prosperous communities and leaving about as much in return as a traveling band of gypsies." Yet what is more American than the entrepreneurial spirit? It's in our nature to think big. At least that's how they thought at Sears until they got so big that folks stopped sending in the mail orders. Wal-Mart became number one in retail, and Sam maintained that was because Wal-Mart kept alive a friendly, small-town attitude. Greeters at the door and all that. Sam set the tone with his pickup and his bird dogs and his aw-shucks modesty. The Wal-Mart style put customers at their ease.

It turned out, though, that more than the customers needed to be put at ease. Just about all of F. W. Woolworth's retail ideas worked for Sam, except one—the notion that clerks, like merchandise, are cheap and expendable. That concept didn't play as well in the seventies as it had at the turn of the century. There were labor problems at Wal-Mart, most notably in Clinton and Mexico, Missouri, where the Retail Clerks Union organized strikes. Wal-Mart management launched a program called "We Care," a "partnership" that included profit sharing, incentive bonuses, discount stock purchase plans, and, in Sam's words, "a genuine effort to involve the Associates in the business so that we can all pull together." That's what the employees were now, Associates, all four hundred thousand of them, and Sam generously emphasized that it was their cheerful commitment, more than Wal-Mart's merchandising, distribution, technology, market saturation, and real estate strategy, that was the reason for the company's success.

As important as the economic incentives was the new corporate culture. "Sure, it's a little strange," Sam conceded, "for a vice president to dress in pink tights and a long blond wig and ride a white horse around Bentonville town square, as Charlie Sell did in 1987, after he lost a Saturday morning meeting bet that December sales wouldn't top $1.3 billion." Pretty corny, but at Wal-Mart "we thrive on a lot of the traditions of small town America, especially the parades with marching bands, cheerleaders, drill teams, and floats. Most of us grew up with it."

Frank Capra's *It's a Wonderful Life* is a Christmas classic, like Dickens' "A Christmas Carol," one of those stories people never seem to tire of. Jimmy Stewart plays a banker who dreams of going off to the big city but sticks around to serve his community. One Christmas, circumstances beyond his control suddenly put his bank in jeopardy. George Bailey, the character Stewart plays, questions the meaning of his life and almost commits suicide. He is saved by a guardian angel and by the townspeople who, grateful for all he has done for them over the years, offer him their own money to keep him solvent. He sees that he was right, after all, to devote his life to such dear friends, who have rallied to support him in his crisis.

The movie was a commercial failure when it was first released; now it is a "popular classic" with an ever-expanding audience. Why do Americans choke up before its sentimentality? Perhaps out of nostalgia for a kind of community that is no longer a reality for most people. Having lost the thing itself, having run away from it as George Bailey wanted to, we forget its limitations and glorify its virtues. We cling to a substitute, the dreamy home town of theme parks, malls, and movies. But then that's the whole point of Christmas:

a celebration of values that have long since vanished from the republic while giving a final holiday goose to retail sales. The taxpayers' half-trillion-dollar bailout of bankrupt savings and loans, a dark parody of George Bailey's redemption in *It's a Wonderful Life,* is our reality. Wal-Mart is our local merchant. Our village is a global village. Some village. Our creations, as Thoreau said, have assumed a life of their own; we have become the tools of our tools. Corporate culture and communities of consumption have at last displaced, almost completely, communities rooted in a place and united by traditions and shared beliefs. Census data and anecdotal reports indicate that those older forms of community, both rural and urban, are in jeopardy.

—

There are those who speculate that the nuclear community of the past, like the nuclear family, is just one social arrangement and not necessarily the best. Malls, they suggest, are becoming "the new downtowns," contemporary centers of urban and suburban life where the problems of the cities—crime, dirt and pollution, the homeless—are, if not eliminated, at least much reduced. Indeed, malls may be just the centers that some suburbs need, those mass-produced bedroom communities (a Zen concept) with names like Apple Valley and Golden Valley (a marketing concept).

That, at least, was the concept of Donald Dayton and Victor Gruen four decades ago when they built Southdale, the first enclosed mall in the U.S., not much more than a snowball's throw from where the Mall of America has now been built.

"Southdale is not the usual strip-of-stores plan," Dayton announced in 1952. "We are planning to create a community."

The Dayton Corporation, the most prosperous retail business in Minnesota, bought five hundred acres of open land, though only eighty-four acres were needed for Southdale proper. The remaining acreage was set aside for an entire city that Dayton and Gruen imagined surrounding their mall. Fifteen acres were given to the city of Edina for parkland and fifteen more to a hospital corporation for Fairview-Southdale Hospital. Starting in 1958, the Dayton Corporation sold lots for single family houses costing two thousand to six thousand dollars. Fallow fields eventually yielded a rich business and residential harvest. When you drive to Southdale these days it's hard to imagine that all that concrete, dense with traffic, was once green prairie.

The Dayton Corporation located its shopping center-cum-community south of Minneapolis because the Dayton brothers saw the city's population moving to the southern suburbs. Southdale's architect, Victor Gruen, predicted that this movement was the pattern of the future. The upwardly mobile professional, he said, "is willing to find his way into town in order to make a living, but he protests vehemently the idea of repeating the nerve-wracking routine for the purpose of pleasure, relaxation, cultural enrichment, or education."

Gruen's observation was more than a casual remark. Mobility and its impact on city planning was the central theme of his career. An Austrian who emigrated to the U.S. during the Nazi era, he settled in Southern California, an environment that would shape itself around the automobile, and shortly after the war he designed a department store outside Los Angeles that derived its image from ramps giving access to roof-top parking. In 1954 Victor Gruen Associates completed Northland Center outside Detroit, the first large-scale shopping center designed to serve the motorists of an entire region. Yet Gruen was far from happy about the automobile, for he brought with him to America Vienna's uneasy tension of historical memory and aggressive modernism. In *Shopping Towns U.S.A.*, Gruen wrote:

> When the automobile emerged as a means of private mass transportation, the final urban explosion took place. Automobiles, free of steel rails or overhead wires, could move at will in every direction. They provided complete freedom of movement to the individual driver and made him independent of public transportation. So, with the automobile came a dispersal of population that followed no pattern whatever.
>
> To accommodate the flood of humans seeking escape from the intolerable conditions of the city, mass-housing builders tore up the ground, chopped down the trees, and removed every vestige of what the people had come to find. Modern suburbia was born, in which there were neither the values of a rural community nor those of an urban environment.

The feeling for human community and the grieving over its loss that suffuses this survey deepened with the passing years. In *The Heart of Our Cities* (1964), Gruen observed that "the urban organism, like the human one, has a heart," and in this heart resides "the urban-spirit, or the city's soul." *In Centers for the Urban Environment: Survival of the Cities* (1973), he took up the organic metaphor again, this time adding environmental implications. He began with a declaration of faith "that mankind will not destroy itself through tools of ecological destruction," despite his recognition that "something is happening, something which we might term 'the unintentional suicide of mankind.'" So framed, his biological analogy became more resonant. "Cities should be viewed as organic structures of a living organism. A city consists primarily of people and exists for people. Its structures, its communications systems, its utility lines, all are means only to serve the needs and aspirations of people. Whenever the mechanical servants of the urbanite start to interfere with human interests—when they threaten and endanger 'organic' (that is, human) life—then the urban environment is in jeopardy."

Southdale, Gruen's heart transplant operation, opened in October 1956 amid much publicity and skepticism. Gruen brought to this project a vision inspired by the arcades of Europe. The first of these was the Palais Royal in Paris. The Duc de Chartres, in need of cash, converted his extensive palace next to the Louvre into more profitable real estate: a landscaped courtyard, one hundred yards by three hundred yards, surrounded on three sides by a five-story arcade building, the fourth side bounded by wooden stalls. In a city without sidewalks where pedestrians frequently had to leap from the path of horses, carriages, and wagons, the Palais Royal offered a haven from the perils and harassment of traffic. It was a self-contained world of galleries, gardens, avenues, fountains, cafes, brothels, shops, and apartments where promenading and window shopping became enormously popular. There was even a "parking lot" for the convenience of aristocrats who were carried by servants to the Palais Royal in sedan chairs. The servants and chairs waited in this designated area until the count or baron was ready to depart. From its opening in 1784, however, the arcade drew people of all classes, and on the eve of the Revolution it sheltered salons, clubs, secret societies, and cafes where politics were discussed and debated. It was here that one would come to sound the currents of popular opinion and it was here that Desmoulins issued his call to arms.

The Palais Royal inspired a host of arcades through the nineteenth century. The most magnificent of these was the famous Galleria Vittorio Emanuele in Milan, its four stories lifting to a glass barrel vault and a central cupola 160 feet high. As its royal name suggests, the Galleria Vittorio Emanuele was the Mall of Italy; it was widely perceived as giving not only Milan but the still-evolving nation a "new center." The king himself laid the cornerstone of the octagonal rotunda on May 7, 1865. The gala opening was celebrated as a national event, lavishly covered by illustrated magazines and described in detail in architectural journals.

Southdale, which was modeled on the Galleria Vittorio Emanuele, also received national attention when it was opened. It cost twenty million dollars and had seventy-two stores and 5,200 parking spaces. Seventy-five thousand sightseers showed up for the gala opening. It was a prototype, and its construction demonstrated that the additional cost of enclosure could be more than made up in the lesser cost of the interior store building, which would not have to be so large or strong. It was also surprisingly energy efficient. Despite Minnesota's long and often brutal winters, natural gas or oil was seldom needed for heating because sufficient heat was generated by light fixtures and the bodies of shoppers; even in January, cooling, not heating, was the problem. Before Southdale, retail executives and building contractors were groping in the dark.

"No one had an idea of what a shopping center was," Mel Simon, the master builder of the Mall of America, has admitted. At the time he was working out of a two-room office in Indianapolis. Even William Kowinski, whose book *The Malling of America* explores its subject with hostility and dismay, acknowledges, "There was an undeniably special quality to the Central Garden Court at Southdale.... All of the elements that would be reduced to clichés in other malls still seemed integrated and natural there."

This was an idea whose time had come. Yet Gruen, prescient in so many of his mall innovations, had misread the future in the matter that mattered to him most. The more he succeeded, the more he was haunted by misgivings. As early as 1962, speaking to a seminar of teachers of architects, he observed that, "With all the improvements that have occurred during the last century in the social environment, that is, in the aggrandizement and distribution of wealth, the physical environment has not proportionally improved but has retrogressed."

"I am searching for form," he told his colleagues. "I want to envisage the modern city as a noble and ennobling place." He never found that Platonic ideal; at least he was never able to bring it into the world of shadows. He returned to Vienna in 1978, where he died two years later. At the end, he denounced the shopping centers he had brought into being. "I refuse to pay alimony to those bastard developments." He had drawn upon history in an attempt to restore some measure of soul to modern communities, but had only spawned a new kind of instant city rooted in neither nature nor culture but in real estate.

The challenge of restoring soul to communities may be one that no architectural achievement, however brilliant, can meet. The dilemma is not aesthetic but political. A community in a democracy thrives only when its members actively assume responsibility for their common life. The triumph of capitalism, by contrast, conditions people to think of themselves as workers and consumers. A worker is one whose service is bought at a value set by market forces. A consumer, on the other hand, is one who is served, not one who serves. Labor and leisure take all our resources. Community service? We count ourselves good citizens if we tune into the news and keep up with "events" and cast the occasional vote. Imagine a variation of Kennedy's clarion call: ask not what your mall can do for you, ask what you can do for your mall. The absurdity of that imperative is why a mall cannot be the heart of a true community, as Victor Gruen had hoped. Yet more and more we see the goods and services of government as commodities we purchase with our tax dollars, and like shrewd buyers we want quality at the cheapest possible price. Some things, however, cannot be purchased at any price. A community of consumers may have stores, restaurants, nightclubs, theaters, a school, an amusement park, a medical clinic, even a post office. What it does not have is a soul.

—

Bloomington, home to the Mall of America, is almost a textbook model of these changes in the character of community over the last two centuries. The earliest emigrants to put down roots in the area—Peter Quinn, an agent for the American Fur Company, and Gideon Pond, a missionary—settled there in 1843. Almost a decade later a township was officially established and homesteaders wove a pattern of common experience: corn picking and husking, barn building, quilting and sewing bees, potluck suppers, shooting matches and horse races, Christmas bobsled rides, tree-hunting parties, decorating parties, and stories told around a pot-bellied stove in the general store.

In 1892 a town hall was built, a structure that adequately served the community's needs well into the 1950s. Bloomington's official history notes that the town "took no particular notice of the twentieth century's arrival." Its "development was slow and steady," though not without occasional touches of drama and a legend or two. At the turn of the century Colonel Marion William Savage, a local entrepreneur, bought a promising pacer. When Dan Patch set the world's pacing record of one minute fifty-five seconds for the mile at the 1906 Minnesota State Fair (the record still stands), he became an international celebrity. Bloomington was still, by the standards of Minneapolis, something of a one-horse town, but the horse was world-class.

In 1950 the city's population was just shy of ten thousand. At that point real estate developers, riding a crest of post-war suburban expansion, ignited what Bloomington would later call "The Explosion": fifty thousand people by 1960, eighty-two thousand by 1970.

"Pastures and fields became instant housing developments," reports the city's official history. "Bloomington was rapidly becoming a solid plane of single-family dwellings, but the wise community leaders intervened." The Bloomington Council adopted a policy of encouraging industrial and commercial development with low-cost housing and shopping centers. Metropolitan Stadium, home of the Vikings and the Twins, opened in 1956, followed by the North Stars' Metropolitan Sports Center. Seventeen major hotels and sixty restaurants mushroomed along a "hospitality strip." The township had officially become a city, and its new city hall, built in 1964, doubled in size within a decade.

In 1961 the National Municipal League named Bloomington one of the country's All-American Cities. *Look* magazine, a co-sponsor of the award, reported that resident action groups working on behalf of the community weighed heavily in Bloomington's favor: "Included among these are the Bloomington Community Council, the AB, Bloomington Civic Theater, Bloomington Planning Commission, Bloomington School Board, Chamber of Commerce, League of Women Voters, and the Sewer and Water Advisory Committee."

The last chapter of Bloomington's official history, written on the occasion of the national bicentennial, is titled "Plateau." Not a good sign. In the land of opportunity, plateaus are where has-beens go to die. Sure enough, in the eighties, the Bitch Goddess let Bloomington know she couldn't be taken for granted. The Twins and the Vikings picked up and moved to the Metrodome, leaving a big hole where Met Stadium used to be. Nature abhors a vacuum, and a free market economy, the most natural way to make money, shares that abhorrence. The city's movers and shakers invited the Ghermanian brothers down from Edmonton to figure a way to fill the emptiness.

There was another hole, however, that no developer could fill. It wasn't a hole that you could drive up to and look at because it was everywhere and nowhere. Let's call this hole "community," not in the sense of a place where the dead are buried and the living stay put, but community as a common pattern of work and leisure, a life of shared values. It was the crater left by "The Explosion" in the fifties and sixties.

Our word "politics" comes from the Greek *polis,* or city. For the Greeks, community could not exist beyond a certain size. Only three *poleis* had more than twenty thousand citizens—Syracuse, Athens, and Acragas in Sicily. Plato ordained that his ideal republic would be made up of no more than five thousand citizens. Once a community gets too big, in this Hellenic view, people lose touch with one another and the conviction of shared responsibility dissolves. The *polis* ought to embrace the whole communal life of the people—political, cultural, moral, economic. Some of those who shaped the

U.S. Constitution, Thomas Jefferson among them, agreed. The Greek ideal of modest *poleis,* however, didn't prevent Athens and its environs from swelling to 350,000 in the fifth century B.C., an epoch of golden achievements and savage civil wars between Athens and neighboring cities resentful of her aggressive expansion. Nor did Jefferson's vision of a democratic republic of small towns, family farms, and local merchants impede the evolution of the U.S. into an urban, industrialized superpower.

Not that big cities, even nations, can't pull together in a crisis. As late as 1959 Bloomington homeowners relied on private wells and septic tanks for water and sewage disposal. When the state department of health found that eighty percent of the private wells were contaminated, the city faced a serious problem. Within four months after the first findings, citizens organized an ambitious plan to create a sewage disposal system adequate to the community's rapidly increasing population. Bloomington is inordinately proud of this effort, a shining hour of galvanized civic action. When they received the All-American City Award in 1961, Bloomington city officials posed in hats and coats before stacks of gigantic sewage pipes, as though to say, "We've got our shit together." Getting it together took a lot of work and a lot of money. The city debt jumped to twenty-five percent of assessed value.

Without a crisis, however, eighty-six thousand people find it simpler to tend to their own business and hope their neighbors do the same. Bloomington boosters, justly proud of their all-American success, didn't notice, or didn't mind, that the city was breaking in two along the north-south fault line of

Interstate 35W. East Bloomington evolved into heavy industry and tract houses, many of them slab construction with no basements, places built in the fifties that became affordable to blacks, Asians, and lower-income whites in the eighties. Today East Bloomington is blue collar and Catholic, or fringe Protestant. Upwardly mobile professionals settled in the newer developments in West Bloomington, where the homes are spacious and the parks are laced with ski trails.

The fault line runs right through the city's school district, with Jefferson High in the West and Kennedy in the East. Both schools field touring bands and football teams, but only at Jefferson are the recreations of the affluent, skiing and tennis, taken seriously as competitive sports. Both schools send graduates on to higher education, but Jefferson, with its foreign language classes and computer-rich programs, gives its graduates a competitive edge. There are social tensions in Kennedy, kids acting out the buried resentments of their East Bloomington neighborhoods. That, at least, is the widely held perception. From the outside it sometimes seems that the only thing holding East and West together is a shared tax base.

The unsightly necessities of this tax base have, by and large, been dumped into East Bloomington. City Hall in the West; Ziebart, Toro, and the fast-food strips in the East. Met Stadium was put in the northeast, as far as it could be from West Bloomington and still within city limits. That is where the Mall of America is now. If you spread out a map of Bloomington, the demographics become clear as a bell—the Liberty Bell, with a crack running through it. It's even clearer close up.

Alice Hanson lives in East Bloomington on 10th Avenue South and 89th Street in a house built in 1954, one unit of a Marvin Anderson tract. The basic model is a one-story ranch with a basement and detached garage. The residents of the neighborhood—an auto mechanic, an MCT bus driver, a construction worker, a retired fireman, an executive at Control Data—have each given their houses an individual character through home improvement. In many cases "garage improvement" would be the more accurate term, expansions to accommodate boats and recreational vehicles. They finished off their own basements.

Alice, who is a teacher, inherited a fireplace and shag carpeting, inspirations of the previous owner. She doesn't care for the shag carpeting, but she and her husband, a real estate assessor, cannot afford to replace it with something new so they are making do, like most of the others on her block. Only the Control Data manager has risen above making do. He moved here when he was just an engineer and stayed on despite his rise up the corporate ladder. His house, the nicest on the block, sports a leaded window and a new deck. There are advantages to remaining in this neighborhood. The lots are generous, and the trees are now forty years old, though the elms are dying of Dutch Elm disease.

Bloomington needs something other than a crisis to pull its disparate people together. Officially, it is the third largest city in Minnesota; unofficially, it is in danger of becoming, in the view of many, two cities loosely connected. What it needs is a center of gravity, a center more emotionally and imaginatively compelling than City Hall.

You might say that the Mall of America is now that center. It employs thirteen thousand people; it brings in business from all over the nation, all over the world. For the first time since Dan Patch, Bloomington has an internationally known winner. The Mall even has its own zip code. The folks in East and West Bloomington now share more than a tax base and high school football rivalry. The evidence strongly suggests that most of them are a lot less interested in how their community came to be what it is than they are in their next trip to the Mall. Do they still have a community?

The Mall of America has what it calls a "community outreach program": a forum for non-profit organizations; space, sometimes in its great rotunda, for community fundraising events. It generously provides giveaways to raise money for worthy causes and is designing a volunteer program to match the skills of its employees with pressing social needs. Mall management speaks glowingly of its warm, cooperative relationship with Bloomington City Hall. But the Mall's conception of community goes beyond the city of eighty-six thousand in which it is located; it embraces the entire metro area, the state, and on occasion the nation. It is, after all, the Mall of America, not the Bloomington Mall. On a good day it contains three to four times as many people as the city's population. Can a center be bigger than the thing it is the center of?

Physically, the true center of Bloomington is its commercial hub, at the intersection of 98th Street and Lyndale Avenue, one block from 35W and thus one block from the edge of West Bloomington. This intersection (which is also the intersection of three shopping centers) was designated in the late eighties as the site of a Bloomington Historical Clock Tower, a symbol that, it was hoped, would restore to the city its spiritual balance.

Early on, Francis Bernes, editor of the Bloomington *Sun-Current,* told Mary Lou Spies, one of the leaders of the project, "If this project is to be successful, it has to have heart or it will be nothing but a brick-and-mortar thing." Everybody, not just the chamber of commerce, had to put something into it. So the Community Time Capsule was created, a whole slew of time capsules actually, a capsule for any person or family or group who wanted one. A fifteen-dollar donation would allow the donor to put a ten-by-thirteen-inch memory packet in the tower; a contribution of one hundred dollars or more would get you a memory box. The full diversity of contemporary Bloomington would go into the Historical Clock Tower, and then in the year 2010, on the fiftieth anniversary of its official metamorphosis from a village to an incorporated city, the sealed contents would be taken out and opened.

The memory packets took hold of people's imaginations. Kids got together in school, each chipping in a dollar to buy a memory box, and they put in notes, post cards, clothing ads clipped from the Sunday paper, videos of themselves doing rap, rock and roll, heavy metal. Kids talking to themselves twenty years down the road. Families, groups at work and at church recorded messages.

The packets and boxes are locked away now and in the not-too-distant future will be scattered back into the city, the occasion no doubt of tears and laughter. Would an anthropologist in the next millennium tease out of them a deeper coherence that would distinguish Bloomington from a thousand other cities of similar size and demographic profile throughout the U.S. in this decade? Are all those voices in the tower a celebration of diversity or a symptom of its unraveling? And the tower itself—a symbol of a community's center or a memorial to its loss?

Let's hope these matters will be a lot clearer in 2010.

Chapter Three

Charlie Brown in the Field of Dreams

"If you build it, he will come."

O F THE FORTY MILLION VISITS made to the Mall of America each year, a third are made by people who travel 150 miles or more to get there. Many travel a great deal farther than that. Half a million come each year from Canada. Northwest, the Mall of America's "official airline," regularly brings in shopping junkets from Europe, Israel, Japan, Australia. The Minneapolis-St. Paul International airport is, after all, only ten minutes away by shuttle bus. Summer is the most profitable period not just because school is out but because the Mall has become one of the most popular places to go on vacation. Instead of yet another trip to Las Vegas or Disney World, you can spend a week at the nation's largest emporium.

Why would people travel hundreds, even thousands of miles just to shop, eat, and ride a few rides? Are five hundred plus stores and eateries a different kind of experience than two hundred? The Mall is aggressively marketing itself throughout the nation and the world, but you might well ask just what is being sold. "Put Some Fun in Your Life" is the official slogan, but surely that can't be it. Everybody is marketing fun these days. Who is going to pack up the family car and head into the vast prairie just for fun?

The secret is knowing how to package fun, knowing the particular shadings of people's desires. Even in a nation as various as ours, marketing experts, their data bases at the ready, are fairly confident they are up to the challenge. One of them boasts, "Tell me someone's zip code and I can predict what they eat, drink, and drive—even think." Such professionals, of course, aren't just discovering our tastes but shaping them. Marketing firms are not paid for prophecies about future trends, however astute or prescient. They are paid for self-fulfilling prophecies. And as movie studio executives will tell you, self-fulfilling prophecy has not yet become a science.

The problem lies in the stubbornly contradictory character of fantasy. In *The Malling of America,* William Kowinski observed that the old main street in his hometown, Greenburg, Pennsylvania, had been replaced by a new main street, Greengate Mall. This was no ordinary main street; it was "an archetypal Main Street, designed to fulfill wishes and longings and to allay fear; it was meant to embody a dream and keep out the nightmare." In his theme parks Walt Disney found a way to make Main Street at once familiar and exotic, homey and glamorous. The visitor to Disney World travels the yellow brick road to the Emerald City only to discover, as Dorothy does at the end of *The Wizard of Oz,* that "there's no place like home." When I was young, that sort of thing only happened in the Magic Kingdom. Nowadays it also happens in the megamall, a fantasy that is safe and comfortable even as it pushes the envelope of human desire.

The Mall: it's not just for shopping anymore. The cutting edge is entertainment retail.

"True entertainment retail," says Linda Berman, a California-based consumer trend specialist, "is like good film, literature, art, or music. It moves people emotionally." Apparently if people are really moved, they "go from the experience to the shelf and buy without thinking about it." The concept here is not new—radio, television, and now movies operate on this fantasy-marketing synergy—but the Mall of America has become a laboratory for new prototypes for a new millennium.

Tempus Expeditions (W 102), in fact, is already swooping customers into that new millennium. A giant bronze athlete, muscled and nude, has been frozen in mid-stride leaping through the plate glass of the store's front, as if passing into a new dimension. Surrounding him, etched in the glass, is Shakespeare's famous speech from *As You Like It:* "All the world's a stage and all the men and women merely players..." Fantasy, reality, two words for the same thing. As you like it. Inside are interactive screens where you can play games or time travel. Whatever you choose, the screen congratulates you on making a "good choice!" There is a theater where, for four dollars, you can go on a wild adventure, if you aren't pregnant or suffer from heart problems or epilepsy. You strap yourself in before a movie screen and get shaken up as you enter "not one of those stories you read, but stories you live in—legends." The story changes every three months. Afterward, still high on adrenaline, you buy a souvenir to memorialize your adventure—that watch, say, with Albert Einstein's face on it. Then on to Starbase Omega (S 318), where you can sign up as a recruit for the Galactic Council. You and your companion, suited up with vibrating sensor shields, fight a duel with laser blasters on the planet Previa or the orbiting Starbase Omega. If your party is a large one, your friends can watch from the observers' gallery, or join the action (the fifty-by-fifty-foot play areas can accommodate teams of ten players each). The battles are juiced up with resonant *Star Wars* sound effects. Afterward the sensor shields are downloaded to computers so everyone can see how they scored. Having "experienced" Tempus Expeditions and Starbase Omega, you tend to think of the universe, with its billions of galaxies, as a delightful, interactive toy.

(I speak of Tempus Expeditions in the present tense above, but it has disappeared from the Mall. It has surely not vanished into the history of bad ideas, because it was on that cutting edge of entertainment retail. Did it suddenly leap ahead of us into a future we have yet to reach, a future where the sales associates are forever awaiting our arrival? Or is it in some other dimension of time, customers and sales associates trapped in a sci-fi story—not one of those stories you read, but one you live in? As they stare at their Einstein watches and attempt to get their bearings, are they thrilled or just confused? Maybe Tempus Expeditions wasn't retail at all but a covert operation set up by aliens.)

Once retailers have packaged fantasies, there is the additional challenge of putting the word out and pulling the folks in. To date, this has not been a problem for the Mall of America. Its public relations are state-of-the-art, and its high-profile success has reaped all kinds of publicity windfalls: a special spread from AAA, respectful recognition from Arthur Frommer, a glossy spin in a vacation edition of *Life*. Trips to the Mall are now part of the booty showered on contestants on "Wheel of Fortune." Four years after it opened, the Mall of America had become, according to a National Park Service survey, the most popular tourist destination in the country.

These wide sweeps are balanced with narrow-gauged targets. I recall walking into Macy's Kids' Department and coming upon loud-speakers blasting music and patter. Sitting at a table were a young woman and a teddy bear of a guy who was autographing posters. The posters said, "Dan Geiger, 1280 AM Twin Cities." I am no avid listener to rock stations in the metro area, but this guy seemed much too uncool to be a popular DJ. And what was he doing in a Kids' Department? I pulled out some paper and jotted down his name and the call letters so I could ask my son later about Radio AAHS.

A man came up and, handing me a business card, asked if he could help. He was good-looking, with a thick head of blown-dry hair, and he was wearing an expensive dark blue double-breasted sports coat: definitely more hip than Dan Geiger. Apparently he thought I was a journalist. Radio AAHS is the only twenty-four-hour, all-children's radio station in the country, he told me. He was soon going to add two affiliates and then "go national." A station that children listen to, parents listen to, he said, and I noticed that adults as well as children were waiting to get Dan Geiger's autograph.

"Why would an all-children's radio station broadcast twenty-four hours a day?" I asked the man with the blown-dry hair. Aren't children supposed to get a good night's sleep? By then, however, he realized I wasn't a journalist and, turning away from me, he once more combed the crowd with his eyes. Over the loud-speakers a voice boomed, "As you move through the world, remember how precious you are!"

I often see Dan Geiger and Radio AAHS at the Mall, a pied piper casting a spell over the children of the town. A mall that children come to, parents come to.

Savvy entrepreneurs are running to Mall management with new ideas for promotion and profit all the time. Consider AppliedGraphics' proposal for a CD-ROM on the Mall of America. In the past, AppliedGraphics in Apple Valley has marketed personal-computer-based multimedia products that are interactive. User-friendly software created for the state of Kentucky, for example, allows travelers at a rest stop to touch the screen in front of them and call up a bed-and-breakfast list for one county or action footage of a resort lake in another. President Robert Bro, a fan of the Mall who frequently entertains out-of-town clients there, wanted to produce a CD-ROM of the Mall that was more ambitious than anything he had done before. This would not be a marketing tool to be sold to the Mall, but a product he would develop in cooperation with Mall management and copyright and market himself.

I sat in on a brainstorming session of the project team. AppliedGraphics had already sold the concept to the Mall's marketing people and now they were working on specifics. They were not worried about the technical difficulties; in their proposal to the Mall, they said, "We answer the question: how can we get the user to the information as quickly as possible while engaging as many of the senses as practical?" They were searching for the most imaginative (and marketable) product design. Bro had seen a piece I had written on the Mall in the *Star Tribune* and invited me to Applied-Graphics to give them some fresh ideas. I had just one suggestion: Tell stories.

They ran with that, but (given their different purpose and medium) they wound up in a different place than I had. Their version of the concept: give customers the resources to tell ("intuitively," a word they liked to use) their own stories. To wit: Ward, June, Wally, and the Beav come to the Mall on their family vacation and have a wonderful time. They want to take something home with them to help them remember and, if possible, relive their vacation. They discover a CD-ROM at the Mall Store (which markets products bearing the Mall logo) that is a whole other spin on the slides-of-our-trip-out-west snoozarama. This is an interactive video that the Cleavers can manipulate in ways that are dazzling and at the same time are no muss, no fuss.

Once home, the Cleavers invite friends over to show them this fabulous mall they visited in Minnesota. You've got to see it to believe it, Ward tells his guests, and proceeds to show them the basketball court and hockey rink at Oshman's,

America's Original Sports Bar, etc. "Wait a minute, wait a minute," June interrupts, "I want to show Molly Blooming-dale's and the Chapel of Love." She takes over the screen. "Come on, Mom," Wally pipes up after ten or fifteen minutes. "When do I get to show Eddie the Virtual Reality games?" The Beav clamors for a chance to show off the action-footage of Camp Snoopy rides shot from the point of view of the riders.

Or maybe they don't hold this family-unit Tupperware party. Maybe Ward has the guys over for the Super Bowl, say, and at half time he starts telling them about this fantastic sports store in the Mall of America. When he is rebuffed with suggestions that he is exaggerating, perhaps misremembering a wee bit, he puts in his CD-ROM and shows the skeptical SOBs. June invites her bridge club over for her itinerary of must-see places. Wally and the Beav ditto. These days the family, like everything else, is modular.

All these friends leave the Cleavers' saying, "Hey, why don't we go to that mall sometime?" Imagine that only a fraction of the millions of annual tourists to the Mall leave with such a CD-ROM and fan out across the country and show it to their friends, and a fraction of those friends go to the Mall themselves and buy their own CD-ROM and bring it home and show it to their friends....

"What about all those Japanese that fly to the U.S. on Northwest [with Minneapolis its hub city]?" Bob Bro asked at one point. "Why don't we propose to Northwest that when they sell the Japanese their thousand-dollar tickets, they throw in the CD-ROM gratis?" These tourists and businessmen go to the Mall and then fly home to recreate their adventure in America's biggest, glitziest shopping emporium. Then some of those friends call up Northwest and price out the Tokyo-Minneapolis package.... Bro has envisioned a global market for this product from the start.

The Mall management has given the nod to the concept of a CD-ROM and is even considering building a large inter-active screen where customers could explore the Mall or see if they want to buy their own high-tech scrap book. Think about it. Wouldn't Dorothy have wanted an interactive video of her adventures in Oz to take back to Kansas?

The Mall, for its part, is in high gear to provide an inter-active experience worth taking back to Kansas. It has assem-bled an impressive menu of our national fantasies. The Mall's foundation was a good start: the site of the old Met Stadium. The Christian Church did that sort of thing all the time, build-ing a chapel on the ashes of a razed pagan altar, taking a Sol-stice ritual and calling it Christmas, gathering about the gospel ancient but still potent associations. So the old home plate is back where it used to be, a bronze plaque now on the floor between Mrs. Knott's Restaurant and the entrance to the Rip-saw roller coaster in Camp Snoopy. In the publicity blitz lead-ing up to the Mall's opening, the PR people went out of their way to remind folks of the rich history of that hallowed ground.

• The first game was played in Met Stadium on April 21, 1961. The Twins lost to Washington 5–3 in front of 24,606 fans.

- The All-Star Game was played at Met Stadium on July 13, 1965, with 46,706 attending. The National League beat the American league 6–5.

- Game seven of the 1965 World Series attracted the largest crowd for a sporting event at the Met, with 50,596 fans.

- Reggie Jackson hit the longest home run at the Met on July 5, 1969. The ball hit the scoreboard.

- The hottest game was played on June 29, 1970, when the temperature reached ninety-seven degrees. Twins pitcher Jim Perry lost eight pounds by the ninth inning while defeating Kansas City 5–4.

- The first regular-season NFL game at the Met took place September 17, 1961. The Vikings beat the Bears 37–13. Early in the second quarter, Fran Tarkenton completed his first NFL touchdown pass, a ten-yarder to Bob Schnelker.

- Vikings coach Bud Grant directed the longest home winning streak at the Met, winning fourteen games in 1969 and 1970.

- The Beatles played at the Met on August 21, 1965, drawing fewer than thirty thousand fans.

- The all-time record crowd for an event at the Met was sixty-five thousand for an Eagles concert on August 1, 1978.

The sports theme reappears throughout the Mall in kiosks, restaurants, and retail. The most dazzling of the stores is Oshman's Super Sports U.S.A., seventy thousand square feet, including a boxing ring with punching and speed bags, a batting cage with an automatic pitching machine, a three-quarter size racquetball court, a mini hockey rink, a computerized video golf course, and a half-adult-size simulation basketball court. Herman's World of Sporting Goods is almost as big. Three of the nightclubs on the Upper East Side—Hooters, Players, and America's Original Sports Bar—broadcast sports events nonstop on ubiquitous television screens. America's Original Sports Bar (eleven thousand square feet) has forty-five television screens, seven satellite dishes, a mini basketball court, a driving cage for golfers, ten pool tables, and sumo wrestling gear. For five dollars, you can put on a helmet and bang away at pterodactyls on a virtual reality safari.

And then there is Field of Dreams, a shop that sells sacred relics: a Twins jersey with Kent Hrbek's number (14) and his autograph ($850). Harmon Killebrew's jersey ($1995). Baseballs autographed by Mickey Mantle and Pete Rose ($79), each with a "Guarantee of Authenticity" by Field of Dreams. Vintage baseball cards. Cold-cast porcelain action figures. All authentic. In fact, Cleveland second baseman Carlos Baerga once paid eighty-nine dollars for an autographed photograph of himself. In the final season at Met Stadium, the combined price of Twins and Vikings season tickets cost $887. Today $800 will get you a basketball autographed by Michael Jordan.

The sporting life, however, does not occupy center stage at the Mall of America. That honor is reserved for a team famous for never winning a game, Charlie Brown and company. Snoopy, that most indifferent of competitors, hovers blissfully over the central amusement park with its twenty-three rides, three entertainment theaters, seven shops, and fourteen eating places.

"You know what bothers me the most," Charlie Brown once confided to Schroeder after yet another humiliating defeat. "I feel that I've let down you players, who had faith in me as a manager."

"Oh, well, if that's what's bothering you, just forget it," Schroeder tells him. "We never really had any faith in you." The Mall of America apparently does.

Charlie Brown, after all, is a local boy. His creator, Charles Schulz, grew up in St. Paul, where his father owned and operated the Family Barbershop at Snelling and Selby. The Schulzes lived frugally in an apartment over the shop; Carl Schulz's only indulgence was the funnies, and he bought four Sunday papers each week just for the comics. When Charles came along in 1922, an uncle nicknamed him Sparkie two days after his birth, a moniker that referred to Barney Google's racehorse, Spark Plug. Carl's only child was educated in the tradition at his father's knee: Lord Pushbottom and Moon Mullins, Skippy, Annie and Daddy Warbucks, Wash Tubbs, Prince Valiant, Buck Rogers. In kindergarten, Sparkie's teacher passed out crayons and butcher paper one day, and when she saw his drawing of a man shoveling Minnesota snow she said, "Someday, Charles, you're going to be an artist."

He could not have chosen a better moment to discover his calling. He and his medium came of age together. Cartoons had originally been used to sell newspapers, as they still are, but in 1902 William Randolph Hearst's *New York Journal* published five titles in cardboard covers—the reprinted Sunday pages in color—and sold these "comic books" for fifty cents. In the first three decades of the century, more and more characters who found an audience in newspapers—Buster Brown, Mutt and Jeff, the Katzenjammer Kids, Little Orphan Annie, Tailspin Tommy, Dick Tracy—made their way into comic books. Movie stars started showing up there, too: Charlie Chaplin, Tarzan, Mickey Mouse.

In January of 1933 two guys who had known each other in high school, Jerry Siegel and Joe Shuster, began fooling around with a cartoon character they called Superman. It would be five years before they would sell their idea to an editor, but right from the start they envisioned the possibilities.

"One day I read in some leading magazine about how Tarzan was merchandised by Stephen Slesinger so successfully," Siegel later recalled. "And I thought: wow! Superman is even more super than Tarzan. The same could happen with Superman and I mentioned it to Joe. He got real enthusiastic, and I walked in a day or so later, and he had a big drawing of Superman, showing how the character could be merchandised on box tops, T-shirts, and everything. In this drawing we just let our imagination run wild. We visualized Superman toys, games, and a radio show—that was before TV—and Superman movies. We even visualized Superman billboards."

Soon after it launched Superman, the sales of *Action Comics* rose to five hundred thousand a month, and by 1941 the magazine was selling nine hundred thousand copies of each issue. Superman was given his own magazine in 1939, which soon reached a circulation of 1,250,000. His success inspired a boom in superheroes: the Arrow, Wonder Man, Batman, the Flame, the Mask, the Blue Beetle, Amazing Man, the Human Torch, Captain Thunder, Captain Marvel, Captain America, Ultra Man, Bullet Man, Starman, Plastic Man.

Not all of these prodigies survived, but it was the Platonic paradigm, not the shadowy embodiment, that was important—the Clark Kent/Superman duality. Inside an unexceptional person, a will to power was itching to bust out.

"You see, Clark Kent grew not only out of my private life, but also out of Joe's," Siegel told an interviewer. "As a high school student, I thought that some day I might become a reporter, and I had crushes on several attractive girls who either didn't know I existed or didn't care I existed. It occurred to me: What if I was real terrific? What if I had something special going for me, like jumping over buildings or throwing cars around or something like that? Then maybe they would notice me."

Bruce Wayne, off duty, was "a bored young socialite." Captain America's alter-ego, Steve Rogers, tried to enlist in '41 but was turned down "because of his unfit condition." Captain Marvel was really a teenage boy named Billy Batson. By uttering the magic word "Shazam!" (revealed to him by a mysterious wizard in the subway), he could become the World's Mightiest Mortal, possessing the wisdom of Solomon, the strength of Hercules, the stamina of Atlas, the power of Zeus, the courage of Achilles, and the speed of Mercury. At the end of each adventure Captain Marvel needed only to shout "Shazam!" once more to return to his ordinary identity as Billy. These superheroes shepherded in the Golden Years of comics, the teenage years of Charles Schulz. Their adventures were a cartoon amalgam of pulp fiction and movie serials, and a figure born in one medium could easily slip into another.

By the fifties, though, superheroes were out of fashion. (Superman, as always, remained the exception.) The decade that fell in love with *Peanuts* was not interested in larger than life adventures. The Comics Code Authority banished sex, crime, and gore. Young people turned from comics to television; they became fans of Howdy Doody, Davy Crockett, Captain Kangaroo, and the Beaver. A lot of these television hits—Lucy, Davy, Captain Video—spun off into comic books, where they rubbed shoulders with Scrooge McDuck and Mickey Mouse. Comics purveyed harmless fun and socially redeeming values. There were even Classic Comics: *Ben Hur, Moby Dick, Ulysses*. Thrills and gore didn't disappear completely; they went underground and bided their time in *The Crypt of Terror*.

But superheroes, by definition, can't die. They are back again, as we knew they would be: Flash, Prime, Timecop, Hardware Company Man, Hulk 2099, Concrete. These hunks are alive and well in the Mall at Tekno Comix (E 206) and Comic College (E 350). Comic superheroes are now on CD-ROM, allowing you to enter the storyline and push it in ever new directions. On CD-ROM, death is never final, only a setback. In *The Cyberplasm Formula,* "Victor Vector and his digital dog Yondo are on a life-or-death mission to recover the secret formula for creating cyberplasm. And it's all up to you. So grab the controls and guide them through the twenty-first century, a world of roving robots, menacing mazes and more!" On another adventure, Victor and Yondo go back to ancient Rome and you have innumerable opportunities to rewrite history. Now *that's* power. It's true that sometimes real people get trapped inside cartoons and die, but the cartoons themselves live on. And anyway, it's the cartoons we love, not the people inside them: Marilyn and Elvis can prosper quite happily without them.

Cartoons are what we have instead of myths in America: is there really such a big difference between them? Stories of power and desire are stories of power and desire. Elvis pigged out on dope and cheeseburgers and nymphets until he choked to death. Marilyn got screwed over by the Kennedys and died of postcoital sadness. That's part of what makes Elvis Elvis and Marilyn Marilyn. It's what makes rock and roll rock and roll. The Greeks understood it. Die young and blaze on in memory: Achilles, James Dean, Jimi Hendrix. Elvis lives.

Charlie Brown knows all this; that's what makes him Charlie Brown. In a 1951 strip, he walks by himself, musing, "I'd like to be president, or a five-star general or a big-time operator...."

Patty and Violet pass him with a friendly greeting, "Hello, there, Charlie Brown," and as they walk away Patty says to Violet, "That Charlie Brown's sure a nice guy, isn't he?"

"He sure is!" Violet agrees. "Good Ol' Charlie Brown!"

A despondent Charlie Brown, once more alone, reflects, "But that's all I'll ever be...just Good Ol' Charlie Brown." Good is not good enough. As Lucy reminds Charlie Brown again and again, ordinary goodness is contemptible as a standard of self-measure. In *Peanuts,* especially in the fifties and sixties, ordinary existence was treated as a complicated problem, as it was in existentialism, a philosophy that was fashionable in those decades.

When existentialism gave way to therapy, psychiatrists put Charlie Brown on the couch. Schulz himself acknowledged the possibilities here when he put Lucy on retainer as in-house therapist. Even the hip guru of semiotics, Umberto Eco, has made a study of him.

> He always fails. His solitude becomes an abyss, his inferiority complex is pervasive—tinged by the constant suspicion (which the reader also comes to share) that Charlie Brown does not have an inferiority complex, but really is inferior. The tragedy is that Charlie Brown is not inferior. Worse: he is absolutely normal. He is like everybody else. This is why he proceeds always on the brink of suicide or at least of nervous breakdown, because he seeks salvation through the routine formulas suggested to him by the society in which he lives (the art of making friends, how to make out with girls...he has been ruined, obviously, by Dr. Kinsey, Dale Carnegie, Erich Fromm, and Lin Yutang).

"Oh how can there be, / one small person as thoroughly, totally, utterly / 'Blah' as me?" he sings in *You're a Good*

Man, Charlie Brown, one of the most widely produced musicals in America.

Odd that his failure, his "blah," has been so successful. The *Peanuts* strip runs in over two thousand newspapers, appears in sixty-eight countries, and has been translated into twenty-six languages. Paperback collections of the strip have sold more than three hundred million copies. There have been thirty television specials and four feature films. The Apollo Ten astronauts named their command module Charlie Brown and the lunar excursion module Snoopy. Retail sales of *Peanuts* merchandise run in the neighborhood of a billion dollars annually. Charlie Brown, of course, didn't do all this by himself. He had his friends. He had his dog.

The burden of longing, of dreaming outrageous dreams, was assumed by Snoopy in the sixties, when Charlie, hammered by unrelenting defeat, gave up all hope of greatness. Snoopy became the hungry heart—which seems peculiar, since every dog I've ever known (and I've known quite a few) has been perfectly content to be an ordinary dog.

For twelve years our family had a beagle, the sweetest, most complaisant animal you could ever hope to meet. A little territorial, perhaps, but very genial beneath his bark. So Snoopy always struck me as a strange choice to carry the burden of destiny, dueling with the Red Baron, composing great novels. I suppose that is what makes him funny. Then, too, freed from the complications of human nature, unmindful of the challenge of authenticity, he can ride his alpha waves into the blue beyond. Whatever the reason, once Snoopy started his dogfights with the Red Baron, he lifted *Peanuts* into the stratosphere. He turned the strip into a worldwide cult; he is the chief impetus behind the billion-dollar retailing. He is the one who floats over Camp Snoopy, blissed out and full of hot air, as big as the Goodyear blimp.

So what do we have, finally? A warm puppy and an ensemble of survivors. There is more energy in comics than in any other medium. From the Katzenjammers to Calvin and Hobbes, cartoon kids especially are manic. But you won't find that mania in *Peanuts*. Snoopy's fantasies and Lucy's aggression are the closest the strip comes to the demonic. What are they doing in the Mall of America?

Maybe they are the Mall's way of saying: sure, we're big, the biggest actually, four point two million square feet big, eighty-eight football fields big, but we're also small. In fact, we're downright cuddly. Oh, we get to bragging sometimes, going on about how we do more business than Disney World, draw more pilgrims than the Vatican, how we pull in forty million visitors each and every year, but shucks, we haven't forgotten our roots. We're still local folks. You'll notice that all the rest rooms, men's as well as women's, have fold-down Diaper Decks. You need a stroller, just ask. We put on a good show, but deep down, at the core, we're a warm puppy. Even a dog's got to dream the age-old dream of power and desire.

Shazam! Captain Marvel. Shazam! Billy Batson. Staying alive. Surviving.

Sparkie Schulz lives out this paradox in his own way. *Forbes* magazine rates him as one of the nation's ten richest entertainers. He's the godfather of living cartoonists. Movie stars call him on the phone; U.S. presidents invite him to dinner.

The adventure comics were his favorite when he was young, and even now he says he likes crime novels "if the hero beats people up and shoots them."

But he has the demeanor and behavior of a veterinarian...a very insecure veterinarian. He has struggled with loneliness and depression his whole life. Even as a child, he says, "I was a bland, stupid-looking kid who started off badly and failed at everything." He suffers from agoraphobia, "a marked fear of being alone or in public places from which escape might be difficult or help might not be available in the event of sudden incapacitation—crowded places, tunnels, bridges, or public transportation." The literal Greek translation of agoraphobia is "fear of the marketplace."

"Just the mention of a hotel makes me turn cold," he has said. "When I'm in a hotel room alone, I worry about getting so depressed I might jump out a window." When it comes to the defeats and humiliations of his life, he has the power of total recall.

Given his agoraphobia, the father of *Peanuts* would be more at home in Mr. Rogers' neighborhood, though he is terribly shy about sharing his feelings. He prefers to work alone, a mild-mannered Clark Kent sitting down to his cartoon board each day to do his bit for the *Daily Planet*. He hasn't forgotten how he started, with the *Li'l Folks* cartoons that he drew in his father's apartment over the barbershop at Snelling and Selby, cartoons he published in the St. Paul *Pioneer Press* before taking them to a syndicate, which promptly renamed them *Peanuts*. Though he left Minnesota for California years ago, he never stopped being a hometown boy.

He even built an indoor ice rink out there on the West Coast, where he goes everyday for breakfast and lunch, so you could say he's got the best of both states. Still unassuming. Like that other Charles, Lindbergh, who grew up in Little Falls, Minnesota, and later flew across the Atlantic all by himself. When he got out of his plane at Orly Field outside Paris and saw all the people who had showed up to shake his hand, he was so surprised that he dug his toe in the tarmac, and all he could say was "Shucks."

I suspect, though, that the days of the aw-shucks super-hero are pretty much behind us. Three of the New Breed—Arnold Schwarzenegger, Sylvester Stallone, and Bruce Willis—have joined forces in a new marketing adventure, Planet Hollywood. They fly in with their friends, perhaps on the jet Arnold was given as part of his package on *The Last Action Hero,* and throw a big party filled with celebs. When Planet Hollywood opened on the Mall of America's Upper East Side, all kinds of high profile stars and athletes showed up. Part of the concept is that even after the opening a Famous Person will occasionally drop in and dine from the utterly undistinguished menu.

It doesn't really matter that the salads are mediocre. The real soul food hangs from the ceiling and the walls: Mel Gibson's motorcycle from *Lethal Weapon 3,* the red convertible from *Ferris Bueller's Day Off,* Freddy's claw from *Nightmare on Elm Street: Part 4,* Bruce's plaid shirt from *Die Harder,* Arnold's costume from *Last Action Hero,* Ray Liotta's glove and ball from *Field of Dreams.* Et cetera, et cetera, et cetera, as the King of Siam used to say. A life-size replica of a naked

Sly Stallone hangs overhead in a plexiglass box (a g-string over his lethal weapon, though you can see the pressure of all that bulk in the fragile loin cloth). The ambiance throughout is In Your Face, a tribute not to Tinseltown but to testosterone. And the food, as I say, is about as good as these films were.

You can't help thinking that there is a deep cunning in all of this. The heavy-handed vulgarity seems to say, "These guys aren't smarter or more talented than you; they don't even have very good taste. They just took their fantasies very, very seriously. And worked out in the gym." The secret of success is spelled out in a "Personal handwritten letter" by Bruce Lee framed and hanging on the wall. (It is stamped "secret," but there it is on the wall for all to read.)

My Definite Chief Aim

I, Bruce Lee, will be the first highest paid Oriental star in the United States. In return I will give the most exciting performances and render the best of quality in the capacity of an actor. Starting 1970 I will achieve world fame and from there onward till the end of 1980 I will have in my possession $10,000,000. I will live in the way I please and achieve inner harmony and happiness.

—Bruce Lee
Jan. 1969

Bruce's "exciting performances" consisted largely of kicking the stuffing out of bad guys. That's what superheroes do on their journey to inner harmony and happiness.

And if you are Arnold or Sly or Bruce, you're bloodied, rich, and famous. But what if you're Bill Travis? On May 12, 1994, Bill Travis, sixteen years old, stabbed his parents to death and accidentally killed his partner in the crime, Todd Thompson, also sixteen. He went to bed and the next morning he left Beaumont, Texas, in the family's Chevy Suburban. When police picked him up two days later in Missouri, they found he had outlined in a notebook an extraordinary path to glory. It began, "1. Kill my parents and family—Saturday 6:00 P.M.-8:00 P.M." He planned to kill the family dogs and a neighbor as well, James Ruby, who taught chemistry in the high school Bill attended. "Kill Mr. Ruby and take van and money he has." Before leaving Beaumont, he and Thompson would stock up on needed supplies, some CDs, a disc player, some electronic games. En route to Houston, they would derail a train and rob a convenience store "and kill victims." He and his friend would "make up everything as we go after this period." Their final destination, Bill later testified in court, was the Mall of America in Bloomington, Minnesota.

During his trial, facing life in prison, he said he was very sad about his mother's death. (He had stabbed her twenty-three times.) Presented with the pictures of her body, he cried. At night in his cell, he no doubt replayed each step of his tragedy. 1. Kill Mom and Dad. 2. Buy CDs. 3. Drive to Mall of America. If he were living in CD-ROM time, he could start over and punch the story in a different direction. Mom and Dad don't die, Todd doesn't die. But the thing is, his life was no longer a menu of variables.

Still, who can tell? The story may get retold in a different way. A West Coast producer reads about Bill in the papers and sets a writer to work on the material and he turns it into a mayhem-on-the-road picture, a surefire hit. Years later, patrons at Planet Hollywood point to the Chevy Suburban hanging from the ceiling and talk about great bits from the movie. Bill Travis may make it to the Mall of America yet.

Superheroes: if you look them in the eye too hard for too long they go wobbly in the knees. Maybe that is what the Mall is telling us with Snoopy and Charlie Brown. Maybe the message is: Nobody is a hero all the time, but everyone is a hero sometime, if only for a moment, a very sweet moment, and these moments are the stuff of dreams. If you believe in magic.

At Amazing Pictures (N 366), they have this amazing camera that fits your face exactly into a hole between Tom Cruise's hair and his *Top Gun* flight jacket, or into a hole just above Bruce Springsteen's biceps and guitar, or into a hole carefully balanced on the neck of a rippling hunk. It's not just a snug fit, some tiny computer or something adjusts the color so that you become Tom Cruise or Bruce Springsteen and you've got the irrefutable evidence right there on the poster or T-shirt or thermos mug (small or large). For the ladies, they have D-cup bimbos with heavy manes. Want to sing to a crowd? There's always Karaoke. You're the next Seinfeld? Knuckleheads Comedy Club (E 406).

Everywhere television screens, whole banks of them, strafe the crowds with rapid fire: in Macy's and Bloomingdale's, in

Bare Bones, in Suncoast, Sam Goody and Saturday Matinee, in Hooters, Players, America's Original Sports Bar, in Oshman's Super Sports U.S.A., in Herman's World of Sporting Goods. In the mirrors, in the gleaming metals and high gloss enamels: reflections of you...you...you. Thousands of clerks in five hundred spiffy stores are lined up this very minute, waiting for a nod, a wink, one teensy-weensy sign that you're ready.

Imagine that Clark Kent did not come from Krypton. Imagine that he figured out, studying Escher prints in his room at night, how to reach down from another dimension and doodle some self-enhancements. He'd still be Superman. When he made *Gone With the Wind*, Clark Gable wore false teeth. Off camera, Errol Flynn couldn't get Olivia de Havilland to give him the time of day. Humphrey Bogart was five foot eight. Paul Newman, Al Pacino, and Tom Cruise are all five foot eight, give or take an inch. The step from the ordinary to the extraordinary is just that, a step, once you accept the possibility of possibility. Shazam!

This is your moment, Charlie Brown.

Chapter Four

Attitude Adjustment

FRANK AND KIMMY pulled out of their driveway early Friday morning. Their plan was to drive Kimmy's LeBaron convertible straight through from Seattle to Minneapolis. Their tight budget had no room for the unnecessary expense of a motel. They had not budgeted for car repair either, so when the LeBaron's engine overheated in Wyoming, they phoned Kimmy's mother back in Seattle to get her credit card number to pay for a new thermostat. The air conditioning had shut down as well, but they were unwilling to have that fixed. They pressed on across the high plains in July heat, stopping in Rapid City to negotiate quick showers at a cheap motel ($15). When they reached the Mall of America early Sunday morning the shops were not yet open, so they caught up on lost sleep in their car.

They had planned their three days at the Mall very carefully. Day one: get maps and become oriented; day two: make a list of possible purchases; day three: make purchases. On that first day they got color-coded maps and began navigating the 4.2 miles of retail, systematically scouting stores on the first two levels, comparing impressions and recording those shops they wished to return to in a three-by-five-inch spiral notebook. At 6:30 P.M., they phoned Kimmy's cousin Lisa to tell her they were in Minneapolis and to ask for directions to her apartment. When they arrived, Lisa and her husband suggested dinner at an excellent but inexpensive Afghan restaurant, a suggestion that dismayed Frank and Kimmy. The two couples went to Fuddruckers for hamburgers and fries.

The next morning Frank and Kimmy turned down Lisa's offer of breakfast. They wanted to arrive at the ramps early to get the parking spot they'd had the day before, which they felt was ideal, and they had a "buy one/get one free" coupon for Cinnabons and were looking forward to breakfast at the Mall. They spent the morning exploring level three. When they reached Collectibles Showcase (W 326), they both knew that this was where Kimmy would be making her serious purchases. Their small fifties rambler back in Seattle is crammed with her collections. They overflow the display cases that Frank has built and cover almost every surface in every room. Her wedding collection is typical: dolls in weddings dress, teddy bears in wedding dress, wine goblets, bells, cake toppers.

When Kimmy discovered a music box in which the figures of Rhett and Scarlett danced arm in arm to "Tara's Theme," she knew immediately that it would have to take its place in her extensive *Gone With the Wind* collection (which includes, of course, the deluxe anniversary edition of the video, though not a copy of the novel itself). She was also certain she would buy a Christmas doll in a velvet dress with fur trim. She knew without question that she would buy these things, but she did not buy them then, because this was the dry run. Frank and Kimmy had realized from the start that impulse buying at the Mall of America could easily lead to heartbreak: on the last day, completely out of money, you discover the one thing you absolutely must have. Then, too, they wanted to draw out the delicious pleasure of all three of their days at the Mall. Frank and Kimmy were celebrating their tenth wedding anniversary.

In their seminal study, *The World of Goods: Towards an Anthropology of Consumption,* Mary Douglas and Baron Isherwood argue that "the essential function of consumption is its capacity to make sense. Forget that commodities are good for eating, clothing, and shelter; forget their usefulness and try instead the idea that commodities are good for thinking; treat them as a nonverbal medium for the human creative faculty." Drawing upon evidence from societies as diverse at the Trobriand Islanders and industrial European nations, they attempt to "put an end to the widespread and misleading distinction between goods that sustain life and health and others that service the mind and heart—spiritual goods."

The meaning of consumption, Douglas and Isherwood concede, is very fluid. "It flows and drifts; it is hard to grasp. Meaning tacked to one set of clues transforms itself. One person gets one pattern and another a quite different one from the same events; seen a year later they take on a different aspect again. The main problem of social life is to pin down meanings so that they stay still for a little time." These meanings cannot be pinned down very successfully by individuals, hence the importance of rituals that bring people together in a shared experience. "Goods, in this perspective, are ritual adjuncts; consumption is a ritual process whose primary function is to make sense of the inchoate flux of events."

Frank and Kimmy's marriage is not an inchoate flux of events, but there have been times when it might have seemed that way. They are an effusively affectionate couple, cooing and touching, murmuring corny endearments: sweetie, honey-pie, lover-face. Neither of them dated until they met at a wedding and fell immediately in love. In some ways they are an odd couple. Frank is six feet three inches, a Harley enthusiast with three machines who makes the pilgrimage to the bikers' carnival at Sturgis, South Dakota, every year. (He has his own collection of Harley paraphernalia, mugs, buckles, photos, a throw rug, Harley T-shirts from all over the U.S.). Kimmy is four feet eleven inches and her health is so fragile she has never accompanied Frank to Sturgis. In fact, they had been on only one previous vacation away from home together, a trip to Disneyland.

Even at home they are not able to spend much time in each other's company. For the first five years of their marriage, Frank worked 3:00 P.M. to 11:00 P.M. as a line mechanic at Boeing and Kimmy worked 7:00 A.M. to 3:00 P.M. as a data entry clerk at an insurance company. Now that Frank is on swing shifts at Boeing, two weeks out of every six they have the same work schedule. Kimmy's medical problems have precluded the possibility of children, a source of pain in the relationship. Instead they have three poodles, two LeBaron convertibles (his is red, hers powder-blue), and their avocations, Harleys and collectibles. "They'll be together forever," Kimmy's cousin Lisa says, but given their working lives it is hard to know just what together means.

That may be what was so special for them about their vacation at the Mall of America: three days of shared experiences. As they moved through the Mall, going from store to store, they conferred constantly, each drawing the attention of the other to a new point of interest. At the end of the day they pored over Kimmy's spiral notebook. Each evening when they got back to Lisa's apartment, Kimmy called her mother to give her a full account of the day. In Douglas and Isherwood's view, they were not simply shopping, they were cementing a marriage.

On the third day, they made their purchases. Kimmy bought her collectibles and a Minnesota Christmas ornament, a mobile for a baby's crib, a Mall of America T-shirt for herself and one each for her sister and mother. Frank bought a pair of boots at the Dew Ann's Too Western store, a Harley buckle, and five Levi shirts in different colors. By controlling their impulses they had bought exactly those things they had wanted to buy. It took three trips to load everything into the LeBaron.

After lunch Frank suggested there was one more purchase they might want to make: a cake topper at the Chapel of Love Wedding Chapel (W 240) for Kimmy's wedding collection. The Chapel of Love is a Vegas-style accommodation where an actual service with a judge or minister can be performed.

"I don't know, Frank," Kimmy told him. "We've spent our limit. You know what we agreed at the beginning."

She was proud that they had stuck to their plan, had done the responsible thing. It would be a shame to lose control now. Even a small impulse purchase might take the edge off their victory. But Frank insisted that she at least look at this cake topper, so she humored him. In a way, she too was sorry to see their Mall adventure end. When Frank and Kimmy walked in, the clerks at the Chapel of Love greeted them warmly by name, and Frank announced to his puzzled wife that they were getting married, again. The day before, under cover of going to the rest room, he had arranged for the renewal of their wedding vows.

On their last afternoon in the Mall, Frank and Kimmy, dressed in formal attire, repeated the words they had spoken ten years earlier. As a favorite song, a golden oldie from the seventies, played in the background, Kimmy was presented with a bouquet of fresh flowers. After the ceremony, the bride and groom toasted each other with sparkling apple cider. They were given an eight-by-ten-inch wedding photo and a video record of the event. All of which put them four hundred dollars over their vacation budget. They did not seem to mind. They climbed back into their street clothes and made a brief honeymoon journey through Camp Snoopy. The next morning they got up early and left for home.

It seems a bit strange, getting married in a mall, even if it is the Mall of America, but apparently people do it all the time. In fact, on Valentine's Day in its first year, the Mall brought ninety-two people together in Camp Snoopy for a "mega-wedding." The wedding line started at Snoopy's ticket booth, snaked around Charlie Brown's Kite-Eating Tree and under the Screaming Yellow Eagle, and as the traditional wedding march boomed from the park's speakers, the couples walked hand in hand into a cordoned-off area where District Judge Richard Spicer waited to administer their vows.

"As we stand here together at the Mall of America," the Judge announced, "we are reminded that there is a place for fun in your lives and you have found it in each other." Television cameras recorded the moment; gawkers leaned over the escalators to get a better view.

"Do you, gentlemen, take your beautiful brides to be your wives, to love and to cherish, to honor and to comfort, in sickness and in health, in sorrow and in joy, and to remain true and faithful husbands to them from this day forth?" the judge inquired. Forty-six bridegrooms murmured their assent. "Come, come," the judge chided them. "Surely you can muster more enthusiasm for such a joyous, such a momentous occasion. Ladies, show your spouses how it's done." Which they did.

After the ceremonial kiss, the couples received a ten-point ride pass for Camp Snoopy and a large heart-shaped cookie from the Mall's merchants. They sipped champagne, rode the Screaming Yellow Eagle, and had their pictures taken with Snoopy, who was himself clad in formal attire. They danced together in the rotunda, and seen from above, all those tuxes and whirling gowns formed a brilliant chrysanthemum, the ultimate valentine. "Look around," Judge Spicer told reporters. "Everyone is happy."

The ceremony with forty-six couples has been repeated every Valentine's Day since.

—

Sally's AA group is made up of women who work at a midsize corporation, mainly secretaries who have always met for 9:00 A.M. coffee. One Friday four years back they reconvened over margaritas after work and Attitude Adjustment, a mock support group of survivors pursuing happiness, came into being. Sally herself has been working on attitude adjustment ever since she was a child. Her father labored on the road crew of the Chicago and Northwestern Railroad and, until he became roadmaster, the family had to move every two years. They didn't have a lot of money, but each week Dad brought home a case of beer for Mom, who was a homemaker of sorts. She washed, she ironed, she read, she played solitaire. Dad did all the cooking; for some reason this bothered Sally the whole time she was growing up. It just didn't make sense to her that a man should make all the meals. Her father's cooking was as deep an embarrassment to her as her mother's drinking.

She formed a picture of the ideal family she would have when she grew up, a lovely home in a small town where she would live forever. Her husband would earn heaps of money and give her lots of babies: six daughters, no sons. That was the only reason for getting married—income and babies. Sally would be the homemaker her mother was not. She would cook all the meals and keep the house perfectly clean; if she drank, it would be in moderation.

Because she wasn't interested in a career, she dropped out of college after just one semester. What was the point? She moved to Milwaukee and lived with her older sister for a while. Becky was married to a policeman who worked all night; he'd come home and fall into bed just as Becky was heading off to her own job. After dark, when Becky's husband was pounding his beat, she was hitting the bars. She drank and smoked far more than was good for her. She would die at thirty-eight, the mother of six kids. Sally left long before that happened. What was the point?

Eventually Sally met Steve, a pilot in the Air Force. Steve's folks had plenty of money and he was planning to become a commercial pilot after he got out of the service. It looked like Sally's ideal marriage, but Steve's mother didn't see if that way. When she learned of their engagement, she tore her hair out, literally, and threatened to kill herself.

"I have raised the perfect son," she told Sally, "and you are not the perfect woman for him."

Whatever misgivings Steve and Sally had about their relationship dissolved before this hysterical antagonism. They married immediately; Sally was nineteen.

It seemed that circumstances connived to frustrate her dream family from the very start. When Steve left the service, he became a pilot for Northwest and then was laid off. He got a job teaching in a high school as a temporary thing, but as the years went by and Northwest never called him back, he and Sally slowly realized that the high school job wasn't temporary. They had a daughter and a son and that was it. Sally had to go to work as a secretary to supplement the family income. They did have a nice house.

Sally worked like a Trojan to keep it a nice house. Steve was willing to share cooking and cleaning responsibilities, but she refused. That was not man's work. She wouldn't even allow her daughter, Bess, to help; she was only a child. Nobody else could do these tasks the way Sally wanted them done. She wanted them done perfectly. If she surrendered control, she might well wind up like her younger sister Jill, a 250-pound slob, twice divorced, six kids and three part-time jobs, a house strewn with garbage. The last time Sally visited her, she pulled out two kitchen drawers and simply dumped them into the trash. They haven't spoken much since.

Bess, an account manager and consultant for a computer software firm, complains to Sally that she can't cook or even wash her own clothes because her mother never showed her how. Sally laughs. When does Bess have time to cook or wash? Every week she flies all over the country on business. She's twenty-six and has recently moved into a condo on Chicago's Lake Shore Drive with a financial planner, but they hardly see each other. They have been going together four years; their combined income is into six figures, but Sally wonders if they will find the time or inclination to get married.

Sally's son Mike, on the other hand, does have a wife and child, though for how long is uncertain. Mike and Amy both have stressful jobs; he's an air traffic controller and she's a lawyer. According to Sally, Mike does all the cooking, house cleaning, and most of the child care.

"The only thing Amy is interested in is her career," she says with sharp disapproval. "She even fills out her own income tax form each year and files it separately." When I ask if that is very different from her own daughter, she smiles and admits, "Whenever I complain about Amy, Bess always comes to her defense." She shrugs. What can you make of kids these days?

That's the reason for the Attitude Adjustment group. Sally says that the AA women see themselves as "in-between," between the conventional gender and family stereotypes of an earlier generation and the free-form experiments of today. Most of them married young instead of completing college and most are in their second marriage. They started out thinking of themselves as homemakers and are now working mothers in their forties, more independent in some ways, more encumbered in others. Their children haven't grown up with the same assumptions they did, in part because of changes in their own lives and self-understanding. There is not a great deal of advice they can give to their kids, or to each other for that matter, but it helps to know that you are not alone and that crises like out-of-wedlock pregnancy and divorce are normal—though not, as Sally might say, *perfectly* normal.

I'm going to the Mall of America with Sally's Attitude Adjustment group to celebrate Pearl Harbor Day, a day when, out of the blue, the unexpected arrived to lay waste to a complacent illusion of security. This is Attitude Adjustment's sixth trip to the Mall of America. It has become their favorite outing, an inexpensive adventure that raises no eyebrows. The point isn't really to shop but to hang out—share a meal, browse, drift. Someday the women want to do the rides at Camp Snoopy and perhaps one Sunday come up for the line dance at Gatlin Brothers' Music City. Tonight they will try out a new restaurant, Tucci Benucch (W 114), drop in at Macy's and Bloomingdale's, maybe do a little early Christmas shopping. There are five of us.

Ruth is ten years older than the rest. She was a doctor's wife for twenty years until one summer, in the mid-seventies, her marriage blew up over an infidelity. Three months later the travel agency for which she worked as director of international tours went bankrupt. There she was, with three kids and no college degree, trudging the streets looking for employment. She found a secretarial job that she still holds. She had thought of it as a steady thing, but just yesterday there was a notice in the latest edition of the Employee's Handbook informing everyone that the firm is an "at-will employer," meaning that her employment can be terminated at any time, with or without cause. Since her second husband is retired, this is not a happy prospect. Fortunately her children have already left the nest and are married, though one is already facing divorce.

Libby's kids, a melded family, are still at home; her youngest son has suddenly announced that he will not be going off to college next fall after all. He needs to find himself, discover what his true interests are. Libby, a very practical person who likes working with a clear agenda, is not happy about this turn of events, but she has suppressed her misgivings and is supporting Chris in his decision. Having gotten married in her teens to a guy in the Air Force, a marriage that fell apart after ten years, she knows it's important to know what you want.

Renee has moved from being secretary to administrative assistant—more money, more pressure. Her husband is also under a lot of pressure. He is a chemical engineer who is striking out on his own at midlife, setting up a company with a partner. Though she cannot say exactly what it is this company does—"It's very high tech; I never understand it when Dave explains it to me"—Renee supports her husband's venture. In the near future this will mean giving up her job and moving to Wisconsin, where the plant is. She's ready for a career change anyway; maybe she'll go back to school and get additional training to be a high school counselor, something she has always wanted to do.

Renee and Dave don't see a great deal of each other right now. He spends four nights a week sleeping in a room at the plant and when he is home they are often working on the house, getting it ready to put up for sale. When they are not working, they often collapse in exhaustion. They sit in the living room and read or watch a video. Nevertheless Renee feels her marriage has never been stronger. Every night Dave is away he calls her on the phone and they talk for thirty, forty-five minutes.

"We communicate now even better than we did before."

She finds it easier to say some things over the phone. Speaking long distance, they have become closer. Renee was eighteen when she married her first husband, a man "who was married to his job," managing a variety store. She looked after her two daughters, did all the cooking and housework, and held down a part-time job. When her husband wasn't working he was showing other women a good time. Renee left him, got full-time work as a legal secretary, and started having a little fun herself.

"I didn't get to be eighteen until I was twenty-six." She went out dancing; she danced "all the time," the happiest year in her life. Two years later she met Dave, settled down, and went back to school. Now in her mid-forties, she has a full life.

Renee's youngest daughter from her first marriage moved back into the house after graduating from college, just to get her wind before the marathon job search. Renee's oldest daughter lives up north in Superior, Wisconsin. She has three children, a son and twin daughters, all with a man who can't bring himself to marry her. He continues to hang around, though, and Renee's daughter, Peggy, allows him to because it is very important to her that her children get to know their father. She feels she never got to know her biological father, a loss that remains an unhealed wound.

Renee spends one weekend a month with Peggy in Superior. Peggy has no car and so Renee takes her shopping, takes the kids to the doctor and dentist for checkups, then babysits so Peggy can go off and have some fun. She wants to support her daughter and give her grandchildren "a sense of family, of knowing that there are people who will always be there for you."

Libby and Sally tell me that they and their husbands have separate bathrooms and that separate bathrooms are the key to a successful marriage.

At Tucci Benucch, ferns and green plants are spilling everywhere. Wooden chairs are hung from great beams overhead, though none of the staff can explain why. An ancient folk custom still practiced in the Tuscan countryside? In one corner, peasant underwear is pinned on a cord. When I was in Italy I spent all my time in places like Venice, Florence, and Rome staring at churches and sculpture and fountains. I completely overlooked the indigenous culture, the hanging chairs, the underwear. I had to come to the Mall to discover the Italy tourists never see. Wow: look at these prices.

We agree to have salads, which are very good, rich with garlic. Before long a juicy piece of local gossip surfaces: Donna and Denny Talbot are separating. Donna and Denny! The June and Ward Cleaver of Northfield. Libby wryly arranges the couple in a single frame: Donna is in the kitchen with her apron on preparing a gourmet meal, Denny is standing beside her smoking his pipe. What could have come between Denny and Donna? Word from the rumor-mill has it that Denny has taken up with Another Woman.

"Men are jerks," Sally announces, and when the others protest that not all men are jerks Sally becomes adamant. "All men are jerks."

Libby tells Sally, "The problem isn't that all men are jerks. The problem is marriage."

Sally meets her halfway: all men are jerks and that is why marriage is a problem.

"Men aren't all alike," Renee insists. "It's just that you've known only one man."

Our waitress arrives and urges us to try the dessert specialty of the evening, a rich custard concoction, and we decide to take the plunge. The four women share two portions and I have one to myself.

The rest of the evening we drift leisurely around the Mall window-shopping. Ruth returns a pair of pink silk pants and some blue knit slacks at Bloomingdale's, where the clerk remarks of the knit slacks, "I returned those too. Tried them on and they just didn't look right." Ruth and Renee browse through some Liz Claiborne things on clearance and Renee buys a white pullover. Then on to Carole Little. The women refer to Liz and Carole the way one might refer to Shakespeare or Keats, shorthand for a creative oeuvre. Ruth tells me that Macy's has the largest Liz collection she has ever seen in one store.

In her book *Consuming Passions,* Judith Williamson points out that consumption occurs in "the context of a society in which the majority of people have no control whatsoever over their productive lives: no security, little choice in work if they have work at all, and no means of public expression." In the area of consumption, by comparison, there seems to be greater freedom. "The conscious, chosen meaning in most people's lives," Williamson concedes, "comes much more from what they consume than what they produce. Clothes, interiors, furniture, records, knickknacks, all the things that we buy involve decisions and the exercise of our own judgment, choice, 'taste.' Obviously we only choose what is available for us to choose from in the first place. Consuming seems to offer a certain scope for creativity, rather like a toy where all the parts are pre-chosen but the combinations are multiple."

Eventually we are back at Bloomingdale's looking at novelty items like a vibrating "stress buster" (raised eyebrows, jokes) and a mitten made up to look like Santa Claus attached to an ice scraper. Renee wants to check out scarves in Men's Clothing, and this is the only time I detect any resistance in the group. Sally says she hates going into men's clothing sections. When I question her about this, it turns out she has put in a fair amount of time in Men's Clothing because she buys all her husband's clothes, even his socks. He has absolutely no interest in what he wears, according to Sally, and she supports this surprising claim with strong prima facie evidence. He has worn the same two suits since 1977, a gray charcoal from September through May and a beige in the summer. He goes to church every Sunday without fail and, without fail, he wears the same suits. Whenever he needs to buy an article of clothing, he takes Sally along.

Sally is a stylish dresser herself and her distrust of her husband's taste is so profound that long ago she asked that he not buy her anything for Christmas. For years they have not exchanged gifts.

"You know Steve's idea of a romantic evening? Driving down a gravel road in South Dakota gazing on the prairie. Seriously."

"Do you buy clothing for your wife?" Libby asks me, and I'm momentarily overcome with the insecurity every man feels when he chooses a garment for his wife. Clothing, so important in feminine shopping rituals, is a good example of how gender-specific the meaning of consumption can become. When a woman dresses to make herself attractive, even provocatively so, is that self-affirmation or surrender to the authority and expectations of men? If the latter, why are men so timid about selecting garments (other than intimate lingerie) for their wives? Most men are indifferent to the tastes of the women with whom they are intimate and ignorant of the specific requirements of their bodies, an indifference that is, from a woman's point of view, a failure of love related to the incapacity to properly value the textures of ordinary life. Apparel is one kind of social language in which men are relatively inarticulate (me Tarzan, you Jane), just as they tend to be mute in the vocabulary of feelings. A man who consistently notices what his wife is wearing and comments on it is as rare as one who consistently listens to her. It may be that women dress for other women because other women tune in, picking up on the connections between moods and colors. From the male perspective, women in clothing stores waste far too much time deliberating choices imposed upon them by the fashion industry, choices that are, in any event, inherently trivial.

"Sure," I tell Libby, "I've made some successful purchases."

The subtext of gender tension disappears when the women enter Children's Clothing. They pore over tiny dresses, comparing styles, examining the details of the work. "That is so cute." Sally and Renee don't find anything that seems just right for their grandchildren.

On the ride home I sit up front with Sally and she muses again about marriage. How close does her life match the ideal she dreamed of when she was a little girl? She's not a pilot's wife and she doesn't have six daughters. But there's the beautiful home, all paid up, and the separate bathrooms she couldn't even imagine when she was young. When she and Steve take a vacation, they always go camping in the woods because that is what he likes to do. Slowly she has come to like it too, neat freak though she is. And sometimes she can persuade Steve to take her to a Kevin Costner movie. For all their differences, they can read each other's minds and meet each other's needs...most of them. Her daughter tells her all the time, "You guys are so in sync."

—

It's ten o'clock at Gators (E 408) on the Upper East side of the Mall of America.

"I was a basket case a year ago," the young woman I have just met shouts into my right ear. "My fiancé and I were sitting in a bar over drinks and he told me we weren't engaged anymore, like he was out of the relationship. Whoa. A total surprise. So like for a long while I was depressed. But then Kelly told me, she said your life is what you make it. If you're down you pull the people around you down. So I completely turned around. I've become a lot more open to experiences and people. I don't judge them. Some people who come here can be real competitive—who's the skinniest, who's got the best body, the best hair. But I think, if you've got an inner glow it doesn't matter how you look. Like those guys Kelly and I were with just now. Are you a college professor?"

"Yeah. How did you know?"

"You look like a college professor."

"No kidding."

"What do you teach?"

"Modern literature."

"Hm. I'm taking courses at Normandale Community College, but next year I'll be at St. Thomas. The thing is, you gotta have a degree. I worked for three years as a legal secretary and I said, enough of this shit. I need a degree. My dream is to be a coach, teach athletics. I was a long-distance runner in high school, best time in my life. That's when I felt best about myself. Or I could be a physical therapist. Are you really writing a book about the Mall of America?"

"Yep."

"What's in it? I mean, what are you writing about?"

"All kinds of things. You're in it."

"Me? You mean, if I'm interesting you'll put me in your book?"

"You're in it right now."

"Hey. *If* you're writing it. Like guys ask me who I am, I tell them anything I want. A guy asks for my phone number, I give him a phony number or my real number. Everybody plays games."

"What are some of the wilder lies you've told?"

"What?"

"What are some of the false identities you've given your-self?"

"Oh...you say, I'm a student at the U, an art major or whatever. Once I said I was a nurse."

"And they believe you."

"Everybody here is into a game. Basically, I don't trust men."

"You just said you've become more open to people."

"Up to a point, sure. We all have our fantasies. Like on Halloween everyone came here in costume. Batman, Super-man, the devil, fairy godmother. One guy came as a hunch-back with a dwarf clinging to his back. It wasn't a real dwarf. He had really worked on his get-up; it must have meant some-thing to him. One woman didn't wear anything but a skin-tone body stocking and hair that came down to her butt. Lady Godiva."

"What did you come as?"

"Myself. I'm always myself."

"And you just want to have a good time?"

"Sure. When I find the right guy I'll get married. Like my parents. They've been married forty-six years and my dad still treats my mom like she's queen. That's what I want."

"You think you might find the right guy in Gators?"

"I'm not looking for the right guy in Gators. I'm just out for a good time. But you can't tell. I met this guy last fall, Kelly and I were here, and he came up and we connected. We spent the night and the next day together and then he went to Alaska the next day. He's stationed in Alaska. After he left I kept thinking about him and on Thanksgiving I called him long distance. I got his telephone number from his mom. Then at Christmas I figured, what the hell, and I bought a plane ticket to Alaska. I figured, whatever happens I'll have a good time. If nothing else, I'll see Alaska. I had an incredible time. I met all kinds of great people."

"Did you really do that?"

"Are you really writing a book on the Mall of America?"

The theme at Gators is spring break at the beach. Some details are missing (wet T-shirt contests) and some details are anomalous (a cigarette girl out of a forties night club), but basically it's a beach party with a disco beat. Occasionally screens descend for a music video or a clip from a movie. A clip from *Fast Times at Ridgemont High*. A clip from *Total Recall*, the scene where Arnold Schwarzenegger shoots a hole through his wife's head and says, "Consider that a divorce."

The four-track rhythm, like a high-pressure storm, garbles conversation at any frequency. Verbal exchange is not the point. The point is Brownian movement, heat dissipation, the Second Law of Thermodynamics. A relentless pounding magnifies hormonal drives the way a laugh track fills emptiness in a sitcom. Disco sex: the same thing again and again and again and again. Is any need that compelling? The place is packed. I'm trying hard to be open to experience, to not judge people—the skinniest, the best body, the best hair—to look for the inner glow.

I am tagging along with Pete, who has been coming to the nightclubs in the Mall since his divorce was made official five months ago. He's thirty-seven years old, a self-employed electrician. In 1976 he proposed to the girl he had gone with in high school, then settled contentedly into married life. He and Wendy did everything together. He spent his weekends working on their house, puttering with the car, taking short trips with Wendy and their two daughters. When Janice and Dawn were old enough, he enrolled them in the local gymnastics program and became a regular coach there himself. Their dream, his and Wendy's, was to have a really nice house. So Wendy got a job as a real estate agent to help build the nest egg. It turned out she was quite successful. One year she closed sales amounting to half a million dollars. They bought a six-figure home and filled it with new furniture.

Just before the living room set arrived, Wendy broke the news to Pete: she and her boss were lovers and she wanted to marry him. A couple of days later the sofa arrived, Pete sat in it, then got up and left. He moved in with his sister, dismayed at this sudden turn in his life. His wife's lover was a friend of his; their daughters had played together frequently. He hadn't seemed a bad guy, a bit full of himself maybe, but charming the way a salesman is charming, and he looked good in a three-piece suit. If he and Wendy were to get married, there would have to be two divorces, not just one. Pete couldn't see that happening. For a year he continued to eat dinner with Wendy and the girls, he continued to do chores around the house, he coached his daughters in the gymnastics program. And each night he slept at his sister's.

Then, on his sixteenth wedding anniversary, he sat in a room with his lawyer and Wendy and her lawyer and listened as the lawyers argued over rights and possessions.

After four hours, he turned to his attorney and said, "I'm sorry, I can't afford this. You're fired." He said to Wendy's attorney, "Give me the papers." Against the advice of counsel, he signed them. He no longer has a house, he sees his daughters every other weekend, and two evenings a week he sees them at the gym. For five months he has been going to bars at the Mall—America's Original Sports Bar, Gatlin Brothers' Music City, Gators. In the middle of his life, he is eighteen years old again. Until his divorce, he says, he could count on the fingers of both hands the number of times he had gone to a bar, excluding wedding parties. Now he's a weekend regular. "I would have been embarrassed to admit this a year ago, but now it seems normal. Is that good or bad?"

We are sitting in Denny's restaurant on Highway 13 eating eggs and French toast at 2:00 A.M., reviewing our night on the town. We talk about picking someone up, getting picked up. Pete says that most of the time when he has gone home with a woman it's because she asked. He drives with a friend and when someone he likes asks if he needs a ride home, he can always say yes. Pete is a good-looking guy in trim shape, shoulder-length blond hair with a droopy blond mustache, and women aren't shy about approaching him.

Usually these women are in their twenties or thirties and are divorced or are getting divorced. Last weekend when Gators closed, a brunette asked if he needed a ride home and then suggested dropping in on a party on the way. They ended up in the apartment of a friend of hers—it was 4:00 A.M. at that point—and just as they walked through the door, she told him she was married. It was a lousy two-and-a-half-year marriage, she told him, and she wanted out; she just didn't know how to do the filing.

"I'm sorry," Pete said to her. "I can't go to bed with a married woman. I've been burned that way myself, and I just can't do it."

For a while he dated a woman, a very beautiful woman, he had met in America's Original Sports Bar (E 402), but it was not a happy relationship. She had been married to a guy who cheated on her rather regularly, and she left him for an abusive lover.

"All men lie," she told Pete more than once. "I don't need a man in my life." Nevertheless, she cruises the bars in expensive, provocative clothing.

Pete even went to bed with a lady cop. Well, a former cop. She was twenty-four and had been on the police force in Pete's home town. After a three-year relationship with a guy, she discovered he was cheating on her with his ex-wife, so she went to his house, trashed it, then banged on his car with her night stick. The city suspended her for unsportsmanlike conduct with a taxpayer. She waitressed for a while, and the night Pete ran into her at Gators she had just interviewed for a position on the Minneapolis police force. They had sex; afterward she told Pete about her failed relationship, that she couldn't trust the guy, wasn't even sure she could love him.

Afterward she would call Pete occasionally just to chat, and then the other day she called to say she was marrying the man whose house she'd trashed.

"I'm engaged," she said as soon as he picked up the receiver. "I'm getting married."

"Steve?"

"Yes."

"Is this what you want?"

She started sobbing into the phone.

We pay for our breakfast. It's 3:00 A.M. Pete has to be up for a gymnastics meet at 8:00. Later he will go to Wendy's (she's living with her lover now; his divorce is still pending) to hook up a television in the kitchen.

Last weekend one of his daughters told him, "It's just sitting there on the counter, Dad. They don't know what to do with it."

Pete called Wendy and said, "I hear you might need some help with a television in the kitchen."

"If you've got the time," she told him. She also warned him about the women he had been seeing. "They're just using you, Pete. Someday you're going to get hurt."

"Yeah," he replied. "Tell me about it."

Chapter Five

Cowboys and Indians

IN DECEMBER 1870, a woman showed up at the shop of a Reno, Nevada, tailor named Jacob Davis and asked if he would make a pair of pants for her husband, a man too large for pants sold off the rack. The man was a laborer, a wood-cutter, so the pants had to be strong, especially where the pockets were sewn on. Davis, not a prosperous man, accepted the work and used the toughest material in his shop, ten-ounce duck twill. When he got to the pockets, he paused. The seam between pocket and pants was the point of great-est vulnerability and Davis had tried without success to develop special stitches to keep the pockets from ripping off.

On the table, he happened to notice rivets which he used to fasten duck cloth into tents and wagon covers. "Heck," he thought. "It's worth a try," and he hammered the rivets into the corners of the pockets front and rear. The next month he made to order four more pants of duck cloth, riveting the pockets and seams. The month after that he sewed a dozen more. There was no style to these pants, but they sold. When he was unable to order duck cloth in colors other than off-white, he experimented with nine-ounce blue denim. In cold months, he lined them with blanketing. When he had sold two hundred of these pants, he sat down and wrote to the dry-goods house in San Francisco that supplied him with his duck cloth: Levi Strauss & Co.

> I also send you by Express 2 ps. Overall as you will see one blue and one made of the 10 oz. Duck which I have bought in greate many Peces of you, and have made it up in to Pents, such as the sample.
>
> The secratt of them Pents is the Rivits that I put in those Pockets and I found the demand so large that I cannot make them up fast enough. I charge for the Duck $3.00 and the Blue $2.50 a pear. My nabors are getting yealouse of these success and unless I secure it by Patent Papers it will soon become a general thing. Everybody will make them up and thare will be no money in it.
>
> Tharefore Gentleman, I wish to make you a Proposition that you should take out the Latters Patent in my name as I am the inventor of it, the expense of it will be about $68, all complit and for these $68 I will give you half the right to sell all such clothing Revited according to the Patent, for all the Pacific States and Teroterious, the balince of the United States and half of the Pacific Coast I resarve for myself. The investment for you is but a trifle compaired with the improvement in all Coarse Clothing. I use it in all Blankit Clothing such as Coats,

Vests and Pents, and you will find it a very salable article at a much advenst rate…

On August 9, 1872, a petition and description of Davis's invention and bearing his signature was submitted to the Washington Patent Office by attorneys engaged by Levi Strauss and Co. It was rejected and revised and resubmitted ten months later. On May 20, 1873, a patent was granted for these waist pantaloons, or overalls, as Levi Strauss called them. Mr. Strauss refused to call them "jeans." Jeans were inexpensive pants that he had sold in Kentucky thirty years earlier, when he was a peddler schlepping from farmhouse to farmhouse with an eighty-pound pack on his back. Mr. Strauss could call them whatever he wanted to. They sold briskly.

In 1873 the company's logo, two teamsters whipping a pair of dray horses in a vain effort to pull apart the riveted pants, was stamped on an oilcloth guarantee that was tacked to the seat of the pants. The guarantee promised "a new pair FREE" if the present one of "exclusive xx special top weight all cotton denim" ripped. In 1886 a second label, also bearing the Two Horse logo, was added to the rear waistband.

In the Depression of the 1930s, cattlemen and horsemen, struggling to make ends meet, went into the dude-ranch business, and their well-heeled guests from back East took a fancy to Western clothes, Levi pants in particular. After the war, the company decided to shift its sales emphasis from cowboys and farmers to young people. The focus of ads was no longer on ranch hands straddling bucking broncos, but on the men and women in jeans straddling the corral fence watching.

Marketing played down the workaday West; there was more money to be made on the frontier of movie mythology.

By the fifties, Levis were being sold through large department stores, and the marketplace had altered the original concept—light blue, shrink-to-fit, convenient zippers. Jeans went Hollywood when James Dean wore them in *East of Eden* and *Rebel Without a Cause* and Marlon Brando squeezed into them and climbed onto a Harley-Davidson in *The Wild Ones*. It couldn't get worse from a cowpoke's point of view, but it did. White jeans in 1960, Sta-prest slacks in 1964. In 1975 company sales worldwide exceeded one billion dollars, then doubled in 1979 to two billion. By the early seventies, demand was so great that a committee of fifteen executives was appointed inside Levi Strauss to reorganize the company. It was decided that the corporation should, in the words of one of those executives, "divisionalize, become another General Motors." Four divisions were established, each with its own production facilities and sales force.

"Though not intended," writes Ed Cray in his history of the company, "the divisions would compete against each other, quite as General Motors marquees—Chevrolet, Pontiac, Oldsmobile, Buick, and Cadillac—compete for the automobile customer."

Like General Motors, Levi Strauss was confronted with the challenge of foreign competition when, in late 1974, imports from the Far East, where cheap labor made patchwork denim and elaborate stitching economical, threatened to drive Levi's fashion jeans out of the market. The company responded to the Asian crisis rather more successfully than

GM. It appointed Susan Fantus, just five years out of college, to head its fashion division. Each year she traveled to New York City, Montreal, and Beverly Hills to take a reading on the mercurial weather of popular taste, and then planned her major spring and fall lines with their two hundred production codes—thirteen models in three fabrics and an average of five colors. Factories scrambled to reduce their turnaround time; some plants got it down to six weeks. Levi Strauss, once a family-style operation, had become a corporate pressure cooker, but it regained its dominance of the market. In 1976, the nation's bicentennial, Levis were enshrined in the Smithsonian Institute's permanent collection on American history.

Jeans, like Coke and Mickey Mouse, had become an icon in America's global hegemony, high fashion not only in Gloria Vanderbilt's New York but in London, Paris, Rome, Vienna, Tokyo. What makes them so American? Perhaps it's their democratic associations. Thomas Carlyle, in *Sartor Resartus,* suggested that if you confiscated judicial robes, uniforms, power suits, the political consequences would be enormous. Try to imagine, he wrote, "a naked Duke of Windlestraw addressing a naked House of Lords." The U.S. has attempted a modest version of this proposal: off duty, broom pushers and CEOs get into jeans. Men and women, elders and children, terrorists and presidents wear jeans. Old money and welfare money wear jeans. Jeans, however, are no longer a leveling garment. A survey of the subtle but crucial differences in denim clothing throughout the Mall of America would amount to a social inventory as varied and rich as a novel by Stendhal or Trollope. At Once Upon a Lifetime in the West, you could buy a pair of "Traditional, Authentic" jeans by Request for $59.99, $69.99, or $79.99. International Chewan jeans are also "Authentic," especially the ones that have holes ripped out and patches made from old-fashioned-looking cloth labels, $138.50. Or traditional rayon cowboy shirts from Atlantic Connection (Paris-New York) at $110. Traditional, authentic Western music is piped through the store.

Just what constitutes authenticity in frontier retail isn't all that easy to sort out. Buffalo Bill began marketing the Wild West back when it still was the Wild West, and he too took pains to assure the paying public on this matter of authenticity. A note in his traveling show's program informed patrons, "Our aim is to make the public acquainted with the manners and customs of the daily life of the dwellers in the far West of the United States, through actual and realistic scenes from life.... The whole material of the harness, etc., is genuine, and has already been seasoned by many years experienced use in their original wilds. We congratulate ourselves as being the first to successfully unite in an entertainment all their historic peculiarities."

———

A couple of years before the Mall opened, Rita DeAntine was selling memberships in Sam's Club, a wholesale division of Wal-Mart that targets small retailers. Rita wanted to go into retail herself and, as she canvassed towns across southern Minnesota, she turned her job into a research project. Something in retail, something with promise; her goal wasn't any more specific than that.

On a back road outside of Faribault, she found what she wanted: the original Dew-Ann's Western Store. If you go there today, it's hard to see it as much of an opportunity. A sixteen-by-forty-five-foot cinder-block building painted a dull red and nowhere near the flow of traffic, a wooden porch in disrepair, a couple of chairs, withered flowers in a rusted wheelbarrow. Inside, half the store is given over to clothes, half to tack. Only a person serious about horses would come to a place like this. Back in the fifties, when Dewey Cates and his wife Anna Clare opened the store, horses were still used to work the farms around Faribault. Machines supplanted work animals in the sixties, but horses continued to be a thriving business.

Dewey's father had been a horse trader of some fame in that part of the state. He had a sharp eye for animals—not just horses, but pigs, sheep, cows, you name it—and aggressive entrepreneurial instincts. Dewey was a sickly boy who suffered from chronic pneumonia until he was six. Nothing the doctors tried seemed to do much good, so the old horse trader turned to the only tonic he had any real faith in. At the end of each day, he walked into his son's bedroom, tossed his wallet on the bed, laughed, and told the invalid to count the money inside. Dewey is convinced that gesture of confident success was what finally brought him around. He left his sick bed and went out into the fresh air and spent his days handling his dad's horses. Then the Great Depression took it all away.

When Dewey left home and started his own family, he didn't become a horse dealer himself, but he managed to have a couple of horses around the place. In 1959 he put together enough money to open his Western store. In the seventies, he and Anna Clare turned the business over to their only son, Booty, who took his nickname from his Uncle "Boots" Cates, a cattle jockey who traded livestock. In trading, "boots" means to even up. If one man wants to swap his work horse with another who has a slightly more valuable animal, he can offer a trade and, say, thirty dollars "to boot." Boots Cates was a colorful, larger-than-life character who prospered at that sort of thing. He gave his nephew his moniker and a pony named Snoopy.

When Booty Cates took over Dew-Ann's, he was also working as a rodeo clown, performing weekends at shows around the Upper Midwest. At six feet three inches, though, he was a fairly large target for Brahma bulls and after eleven years he finally had to give it up: too hard on the back, too little pay. But he continued to travel to rodeos to sell Western clothing, dividing his time between home and the road.

When Rita DeAntine walked into Dew-Ann's Western store with her sales pitch for Sam's Club, she saw this big lug in a Stetson, jeans, and boots chewing Copenhagen. He got up, introduced himself and his two dogs, Willie and Wayland, showed her his inventory, and gave her the worst cup of coffee of her life. She sold him a membership in Sam's Club, and when she left she knew: this was what she had been looking for. She didn't know squat about Western fashions, much less about horses, but she knew Garth Brooks was big on the radio and she knew Booty Cates was the genuine article. She came

back several more times to chat with Booty and drink his God-
awful coffee.

Booty was at a rodeo in Granite Falls, Minnesota, on a
hot July night when the phone in his motel room yanked him
out of sleep. It was 1:00 A.M. "We can open a Dew Ann's in
the Mall of America," Rita told him, "but all we've got is a
month to do it. What do you say?"

"Sure enough," Booty replied.

He had the contacts; she had the cash. They negotiated.
She bought the Dew-Ann's name and signed him on to be the
store's manager. Their location in the Mall turned out to be
propitious, catty-corner from Gatlin Brothers' country-western nightclub and perched above Paul Bunyan's Log Chute
in Camp Snoopy. A symbiosis developed in which Dew Ann's
provided Gatlin Brothers' staff with their uniforms (Stetson,
bib shirt, jeans, boots) and contributed prizes for the dance
events, and in turn the Gatlin Brothers crowd (crowds, actually; it quickly became very popular) gave their business to
Dew Ann's. First-time explorers of the country-western scene,
discovering that a Stetson, a western shirt and bolo tie, jeans
and boots are de rigueur, scurried to Dew Ann's Too for the
necessary apparel. An improvised arrangement was worked
out whereby customers could immediately climb into their
Western gear and leave their street duds at the store to be
picked up a day or two later. Starting around 5:00 P.M. on
weekends, the place was always packed.

The principle of low overhead, fundamental to the original Dew Ann's, ruled here as well. The Mall store was about
as spacious as a rodeo clown's barrel. Boxes of Bailey Stetsons

were stacked from floor to ceiling along three sheet-rocked walls. A modest mirror stood in one corner. Boots were hung from peg boards. The jeans were Wranglers, the only pants for real cowboys, because the company is a long-time and generous sponsor of horse shows and rodeos.

In its first year, Dew Ann's Too grossed more than a million dollars, and before the year was out a second Dew Ann's Too opened in Burnsville Mall. A few months later a third opened in Rosedale Mall, and Ridgedale Mall was making overtures. The new stores had more space, more color and chrome, more mirrors. In Burnsville, Rita simply moved her inventory into the decor created by the previous occupant, D. B. Dalstrom's women's apparel. One or two frontier touches—an old bridle, a rusty two-handed saw—are the last vestigial remains of Dew Ann's Faribault ancestry.

A year after she launched Dew Ann's Too, Rita, an attractive blonde with blow-dried hair, five feet two inches and snug in her jeans, was still studying the mysteries of her success. She confessed that she saw no rhyme or reason to the way people spend money the way they do. Almost all her business, she said, came from impulse buying, customers purchasing not what they needed but what they wanted, prompted by a mood or perhaps a recent divorce. A high roller now, Rita carried around a lot of anxiety, but she said the uncertainty made her life interesting.

And Booty Cates? Before Dew Ann's Too opened in the Mall of America, he averaged thirty rodeos a year; in '93 he was down to six. He had an apartment in Bloomington, though he was skeptical of life in the city, its fast pace and anonymity. He spoke of rodeo people as his real community; the word he used was "family." His rodeo friends were the folks he trusted and loved. His time on the circuit, he said, was the best time of his life. A year after the Mall opened, he told me there were only three places he had been to: Dew Ann's Too, the nearest men's room, and the parking lot. He was making more money, though. No question about it.

Two years after the Mall opened, Booty was back in the original Dew Ann's in Faribault. I dropped in late one bitterly cold January day for a cup of his infamous coffee. He told me he had resigned as manager of Dew Ann's Too in the megamall. He had to. The Faribault store had been empty of inventory and customers for too long. Saving it meant cutting free of the Mall of America store, something Booty was only too happy to do. Faribault was where he belonged.

He quit at the Mall in August and put in a couple of months restocking and sprucing up his Faribault shop. Between Thanksgiving and Christmas of 1994, he did more business than he had ever done in his life. Three hundred pairs of boots, more shirts and pants than he could count offhand. He had also re-established his contacts in the rodeo circuit and scheduled the year ahead: three shows in February, two in March, then beginning in April three weekends on the road every month. He was back with his people, horse people.

"I don't know," he mused. "I just can't live in the city. The first year was great because everything was new, but after that...it's just not my kind of life. And working in the store took up my whole week, clerking, punching a computer. I had to get my life back."

Then, too, something was going on fiscally that just did-n't make sense. "We were selling hand over fist but the store kept going into debt. I couldn't figure it. Mike told me I best pull out, so I did."

Mike is a corporate lawyer in Tulsa, Oklahoma, a child-hood friend and a fellow horse enthusiast. Three weeks after Booty left, Rita closed the stores in Burnsville and Rosedale Malls. "I'm no accountant, but when numbers don't add up, I get real uncomfortable." Not long after we spoke, the Mall of America store closed as well. What began as an impulse and fed on impulse perished as quickly.

So Booty now is back where he does feel comfortable, where he doesn't need a software program to keep track of the inventory: eyeballing does just fine. Not that software is a bad thing. In fact, he got a kick out of learning how to use it. But software doesn't pay your vendors. A Western store is more than a concept. It's a way of dealing with people, knowing when to push trust and when to pay up. That's not something you learn overnight. It's how you live your life, in big things and in small. Coke, for instance. A true horseman will always drink Coke over Pepsi because Coke is a gener-ous sponsor of rodeos and horse shows, whereas Pepsi is a big supporter of animal rights and is aligned with critics of rodeos. You can't put on a way of life the way you put on a pair of pants.

Booty learned that living in Bloomington and working at the Mall. It just didn't fit. After two years, he still had not explored the Mall itself. The parking ramp, the rest room on level three, Gatlin Brothers, and Dew Ann's Too exhausted his points of reference. When a customer asked how to get to Macy's, he shrugged. Macy's was off his range.

————

Real cowboys constitute only the tiniest fraction of the market for Western fashion. When we think of jeans, we think of the frontier, a landscape of minimum social control and maximum self-definition. But that association is problematic. In his celebration of the counterculture movement, *The Greening of America,* Charles Reich wrote that "Jeans make one conscious of the body, not as something separate from the face, but as part of the whole individual"; they are "a declaration of sensuality, not sensuality-for-display as in Madison Avenue style, but sensuality as part of the natural in man."

Au contraire, Charles. Wrangler ads promise jeans that "give you the shape you want...a great shape that is all yours," and the ads for Sergio Valente's jeans claim that their seductive pants express "the way you live and love." In a recent innovation on this theme, a few Levi stores now offer jeans made-to-order via computer. I guess that is what the counterculture movement meant back in the sixties when it warned that revolutionary strategies are "co-opted" by the establishment. The sort of thing that happened to Hell's Angels. At Boogies Diner in the Mall (S 320), they've set up a Harley Davidson and are selling jeans and denim jackets turned out in baroque biker style. Prison Blues, jeans turned out by Oregon inmates, sell for as much as seventy dollars a pair in Japan. "Gangsta Jeans," part of the "Gangsta Style."

When the fashion industry appropriated torn jeans, worn-through jeans, some left-leaning critics of popular culture saw the possibility of a social statement, an acknowledgment that the social fabric is by no means seamless. One such critic has argued that children from affluent homes who wear torn jeans are displaying a symbolic "rejection of affluence" that may not quite "forge a cultural allegiance with the economically poor" but does "signify a sympathy toward the situation of the poor." Maybe, but Macy's sees it differently. "Expressions—Faded attraction...the worn out jeans from Calvin Klein Sport...Worn out in all the right places, brand new jeans slip on with the look and feel of old favorites. And when Calvin's cool white crew neck is added (a soon-to-be new favorite) you're set for a totally relaxed mood."

No matter where a biker or a cowpoke or a gunslinger rides these days on the frontier of fashion, the marketing folks have gotten there first and have set up to sell him a song and dance. There are no more territories to light out for, Huck.

When I moseyed on down to the Original Levi Store (S 112) I discovered once more that tradition is a Heraclitean stream. From floor to ceiling along the walls were Levis in a rain forest of colors: olive green, apple green, some kind of coral green (I guess), rose red, deep red, purple, varieties of blue I don't have names for, beige, blond, white, three or four shades of gray, black, all with the Two-Horse logo on the back. As I stood gazing at the inventory, I was suddenly surrounded by six young women dressed in identical blue rayon jackets and speaking in tongues. It turned out they were precision ice skaters from Poland who had come to the Cities for a competition. Naturally they had to see the Mall of America and naturally they had to buy Levis to take home, eleven pairs in ten minutes, black, beige, red, white, and blue. As they sent a clerk up and down a ladder for the right sizes, the rock group U2, larger than life and dressed in jeans, proclaimed revolution from nine huge television screens. T-shirts in the corner proclaimed, "One World is enough for All of Us (one pair of jeans is not)." In that world jeans mean anything, everything, nothing. That's why they are an American icon.

———

At Grand Casino (N 252) in the Mall of America, "The Mille Lacs Band of Ojibwe Welcomes You" with an invitation to sit down to blackjack, video poker, video slots, video craps. No money changes hands because off-track betting is illegal at the Mall, but a dealer will give you a stack of five-dollar and twenty-five-dollar chips and introduce you to the basics of blackjack. There is a display of antique slots from the twenties and thirties as well as a miniature mockup of the two Grand Casinos on the Ojibwe reservation a little more than an hour north of the cities. At Grand Casino Hinkley "90 thousand square feet of excitement" await you, "over one thousand five hundred Video Slots, 52 Blackjack tables, High-Stakes gaming area, and the highest percentage of progressives within one thousand miles!" And as the publicity literature points out, "That's just for starters." Another mockup previews the coming attractions: an eighteen-hole golf course, tennis courts, a small theme park with one of those British hedge labyrinths, an indoor family entertainment center with a child-care facility, a three-hundred-room hotel, and three motels. The RV resort is already in place. Why waste money on a cruise to the Virgin Islands?

On a billboard on one of the feeder roads to the Mall, the Dakota tribe extends an invitation to its Mystic Lake Casino. "We're not as big as the Mall of America, but we're close…just 20 minutes away." That is more than a coy come-on. The casino opened a few months before the Mall of America did. The close proximity of reservation gambling to the Mall has produced a powerful marketing symbiosis and has dramatically increased the number of tourists coming into the Twin Cities. In 1996, Northwest World Vacations booked seven thousand Mall of America package tours, all of which included a side trip to Mystic Lake Casino, the state's second-most popular tourist attraction with an estimated 5.2 million visitors annually.

One Thanksgiving there was a big advertisement for the Dakota Sioux Mystic Lake Casino in the Minneapolis *Star Tribune,* a photograph of a man's huge belly bursting through his shirt, his hand gripping a white napkin.

"One time we can guarantee you'll go home with more than you came with," the ad promised. "The $8.95 Thanksgiving Buffet. We'll be stuffing more than turkeys this Thursday, from 11:00 A.M. to midnight. Because like any Thanksgiving meal, ours will be all you can eat. And then some. Mystic Lake's Thanksgiving Buffet. The more the merrier." Was this the Dakotas' sly parody of Squanto's openhandedness and the Pilgrims' feast, a lampoon of grade-school history?

The reservations used to be the most economically depressed pockets in the state. Now the Native Americans are building schools and sending their kids to college, financing real homes, and launching businesses. People grumble about a trick in the law that makes off-track betting illegal everywhere except on Native American reservations. The Ojibwe and the Dakota have a billion-dollar bonanza, tax free. Yet it seems a just recompense. The Mall of America squats on land that once gave sustenance to a Dakota community.

Perhaps the Dakota lost their territory because they never thought of it as a possession. Can you rightly say a people have settled a place if they keep moving around, the way the Dakotas did when they lived here more than two hundred years ago? They had skin-covered lodges that they dismantled and carried with them as the seasons changed, wintering in wooded bottomland near the Minnesota River, breaking camp and moving to the groves of sugar maple in the spring, on to a different campsite in summer where they could raise crops and harvest wild berries, then off to gather wild rice along the lake shores, then back to harvest corn, beans, squash, and pumpkin.

The Europeans built solid houses and hunkered down on the earth. The first settler made his own bricks for a square, sturdy place that had a sitting room. That house is still standing. When Rene Baillif bought Joe Batchelor's one-room place on Nine Mile Creek, he hauled it onto a larger water cistern and added a second story and then, as his family grew, he built a living and dining area, a front-room parlor, a rear bedroom, a summer kitchen, an upper story with three large bedrooms. That house stayed put. A man builds a house like that, he says to the world, "This land is mine." A man who sets up poles and skins says something else.

The earliest emigrants to put down roots in what would become Bloomington enjoyed friendly relations with their Dakota neighbors. Peter Quinn, who had been taken from Ireland by a party of British sailors when he was a boy, lived among the Esquimaux Indians in the Hudson Bay area for three years. In 1824 he made his way into Minnesota territory, and a year later he was joined by his mixed-blood wife, who came on snowshoes to Crow Wing on the upper Mississippi where Quinn met her and took her to Fort Snelling. For years he worked as an agent for the American Fur Company, and then, in 1843, he was appointed "Indian Farmer" and took up residence in what would be Section 14 of a later Bloomington township. He started teaching a local Dakota band the rudiments of European farming, and because he spoke their language, as the settlement grew he would frequently serve as translator and mediator. In 1862, when mediation failed disastrously, he was one of the fatalities.

Gideon Pond, an Indian missionary, was the other white settler to come to Bloomington territory in 1843. He too learned to speak Dakota, and he created an Indian school. He brought together Dakota children and his own children, then added the children of other early emigrants. Bloomington is now able to boast that before there was a town, there was a school and a church. Though Pond attempted in his role as missionary to convert the Dakota to the Christian faith, he was sympathetic to their culture and worked to ensure its survival.

In this he found an ally in the great Dakota chief, Cloudman, who had grown up among the Mdewakanton near the mouth of Nine Mile Creek. Cloudman's brother, Eagle Help, was a respected medicine man, and Cloudman himself never abandoned the worship of Wakan, but he was persuaded by Gideon Pond's arguments that the Dakota ought to give up hunting and gathering for agriculture. A fierce warrior whose resolution in combat had lifted him to the rank of chief, Cloudman spoke once of bringing back from battle the young son of an enemy and burning him alive: "Our hearts are strong and such things cannot move us." Yet he became a great peacemaker, honored by his own people and by whites. One of his daughters, Hushes the Night, married a trader named Daniel Lamont, and his other daughter, Stands Like Spirit, became the wife of Captain Seth Eastman of Fort Snelling. The only child of Stands Like Spirit and Captain Eastman, a daughter named Mary Nancy, became the bride of Wapeton Chief Many Lightnings after a courtship that passed into legend, a story retold often around fires in the territory.

Interracial marriages were not rare—at mid-century mixed-bloods or "breeds" comprised roughly fifteen percent of the Dakota reservation population and had a substantial influence in Dakota Councils—but the relations between natives and whites could hardly have been further from connubial bliss. In the Treaty of 1851, which took from the Dakota their best hunting grounds and confined them to Minnesota reservations where land was parceled out and the tribal structure broken up, the first article states, "It is stipulated and solemnly agreed that the peace and friendship now so happily existing between the United States and the aforesaid bands of Indians, shall be perpetual." Warriors who mounted forays against the Ojibwe, traditional enemies of the Dakota, were punished, and when officials from the Office of Indian Affairs distributed subsidies, farmers received extra amounts and hunters walked away with empty hands. The authority of medicine men was disparaged by whites proclaiming the Christian gospel. Even clothing and hair styles changed.

In exchange for this diminution of their heritage, the Dakota became economic hostages to exorbitant prices in traders' stores and entered the permanent bondage of buying on credit. The traditional tribal structures of education gave way to schools that did not get built and teachers who seldom showed up. An infestation of cutworms laid waste to the fall harvest of 1861, and by late spring of 1862 Indians were starving. On August 4, warriors broke into a warehouse at the Yellow Medicine Agency and were driven off by a detachment of Minnesota militia threatening the use of a cannon. Small hunting and war parties began to range beyond the reservations. One of these parties came upon a settler, Robinson Jones, near the small community of Acton. An altercation developed, and the warriors killed Jones and several members of his family. Six weeks later, twenty-three southwestern Minnesota counties were virtually depopulated and most of the six thousand residents of the reservations who had not fled westward were incarcerated or executed.

Peter Quinn had been killed early in the conflict. Cloudman had died in Fort Snelling, where he and other noncombatants had been held in a larger encampment. He was buried in the fort. Samuel Pond, Gideon's brother, wrote of him, "He was a man of superior discernment and of great prudence and foresight. He did not hesitate to tell the Dakota that the time had come when nothing but a change in their mode of life could save them from ruin, yet they were slow to adopt his new notions."

Gideon Pond followed his good friend in death fifteen years later. Belle Pond St. Martin recalled that her mother Agnes used to tell her that, when her grandfather died, Dakota mourners came to the house to pay their respects. They had lost, they said, a great friend.

In August 1992, Belle Pond St. Martin's son, Richard, spoke at a meeting conducted by the City of Bloomington and the Minnesota Historical Society to study the possible reuse of the historic Pond House. Sitting in the audience was Gary Cavender, the great-great-grandson of Cloudman and president of the Dakota Society. When Richard St. Martin had finished speaking, Cavender stood up and said he had to shake his hand.

"It was an impromptu thing for me," Cavender later told a reporter for the Bloomington *Sun-Current.* "When I heard he was the great-grandson of Pond, I just felt a need to shake his hand."

It was a cold, cloudy Friday, the end of Indian summer, when I found my way to Scott Hall, the American Studies building at the University of Minnesota, and located the small wing that houses the offices of the American Indian Studies

Program. A secretary directed me to "Reverend Cavender's" office. Reverend Cavender?

There he was, waiting for me, a handsome man in his fifties with a thick head of gray hair. He was dressed in Western boots, blue polyester pants, and a Western shirt. Seated next to him was a younger man in denim, jet-black hair pulled back in a ponytail; he could have played a supporting role in *The Last of the Mohicans*. Reverend Cavender introduced him as brother Tom.

When I inquired about his title, Cavender said he was an Episcopal priest, now medically retired. I noted the aluminum walking brace he held as he sat, but he told me the cause of his medical retirement was post-traumatic stress disorder, one consequence of his work in a street mission in South Minneapolis. Marriage counseling, drug and alcohol counseling, time in court trying to prevent people from being evicted from their homes, work with gangs, cults. He seemed relaxed and at ease now.

He had been working in missions—Native American parishes—all his professional life. "How did Cloudman's great-grandson become an Episcopalian priest?" I asked. He smiled and prefaced his story with the observation that he didn't consider himself to be a Christian. He had greater affinity to American Indian beliefs. American Indian, not Native American, was the term he used.

As a young man recently married, he began attending an Episcopal mission headed by a Lakota deacon with two years of seminary training.

"Can you read?" the deacon asked.

"Sure," Cavender told him. "I have a B.A. degree. You can't get a B.A. degree unless you can read at an eighth-grade level."

"Fine," said the deacon. "You'll be my lay reader."

This was at the All Saints mission on 31st Street in Minneapolis. It was a small parish then. After a year the deacon went back to seminary for another year and ordination.

"You're in charge of the mission," he told Cavender.

A year later he returned and told him, "Now it's your turn." Cavender, his wife, and their seven foster children headed to the interdenominational United Seminary in New Brighton.

A young woman came into the office. Cavender waved her forward with a fatherly demeanor and she handed him a small white envelope.

"These are the pictures," she said, and removed some snapshots.

"So that's your grandmother?"

"Yes."

"That's you?"

"Yes."

You could tell she was proud to be showing him these photographs. Cavender told her about an Eastern Cherokee Travel Center that could help her trace her family lineage.

"You'll likely find your people in the eastern Carolinas," he said.

When she was gone, Cavender returned to his story. He loved his years at the seminary. His academic advisor was a rabbi, his peace studies professor a Buddhist monk. The real learning, though, took place not in classrooms but in the refectory, long discussions with fellow seminarians—feminists, Lutherans, Methodists, Episcopalians, Reformed Mormons, even an atheist.

He was ordained and went back into mission work. They were always missions because American Indians were too poor to have self-supporting churches. He wasn't your typical Episcopalian priest. He would perform Christian weddings but would also use Dakota rituals to bless houses and cleanse spirits. He wasn't a priest really, more a Wicasta Wkan, a holy man.

"What makes someone a holy man?" I asked.

He chuckled and shook his head. Did the fact that he was a descendent of Cloudman incline people to see him in that role? His lips pursed dismissively. Why would that be pertinent?

"Does a holy man build a following the way an itinerant preacher does in the Baptist South, by witnessing in public?" I suggested.

"Nope."

"What distinguishes a holy man, then?"

"He seems to give good advice," Cavender said. "Word gets around."

Guessing that the significance of this might be lost on me, he added, "Isn't that pretty much how the Hebrews decided which prophets to put in their Bible?"

Prophecy: good advice to carry with you into exile. I asked about the Dakota diaspora.

"Are there true Dakota communities in the region?"

"Oh yes," he assured me, "four of them." And he proceeded to identify them in terms of location and casino: the Upper Sioux at Granite Falls, Firefly Casino; the Lower Sioux at Redwood Falls, Jackpot Junction; Prior Lake Sioux, Mystic Lake Casino; Prairie Island Sioux, Treasure Island Casino.

This brief litany clearly delighted Cavender; he relished the ironies. Several years before the Mystic Lake operation was started, the Prior Lake reservation, where he lives, sued the city of Prior Lake to receive basic services—water, sewage, garbage collection, fire protection. The city claimed it had no such obligations to the Dakota community. The case went to the Supreme Court, which decided that the City of Prior Lake did indeed have those obligations. Now, more than a decade later, the Mystic Lake Casino is the biggest employer in the area. The Prior Lake Dakotas have joined in partnership with Prior Lake and neighboring Shakopee to develop an industrial park. They are working with the American Indian Opportunity Council to employ urban Indians in the Mystic Lake bonanza.

Not everyone is pleased with these developments. A citizen of Prior Lake brought suit against the reservation, charging that the Mystic Lake searchlights, which form an electromagnetic tepee at night, violate the airspace above his property. He said he was going to court "to get the moon and stars back." Apparently it did not occur to him to bring his complaint to the tribal council. Similar objections have been made by those living close to the Mall of America. The well-lit parking ramps have, in the view of at least one

137

resident, turned the immediate vicinity into "the land of the midnight sun."

The tangled legal issues here may be without precedent. Do individual property owners have an implied claim to the heavens directly above their real estate? (Technical questions: What does "directly" mean in the context of a curved space-time continuum? What does "above" mean in a de-centered universe? Astrophysicists from Cal Tech and MIT, called in for expert testimony, dazzle the jury with elaborate blackboard equations.) Ought every citizen be guaranteed "fair and reasonable access" to the moon and the stars? Can these matters be legislated by states, or do they fall more properly under federal jurisdiction? (Geeks in the NASA program, their jobs axed by government budget cuts, enter top law schools, invest in power suits and Rolex watches, geeks no more.) The Prior Lake Reservation and the City of Prior Lake may find themselves once again before the Supreme Court in landmark litigation. "No, it's not the plumbing, your Honor. It's the moonlight."

Not all the problems arising from the casinos are amusing. Consider the unsettling case of Susan Robinson, age forty-one, a clerk in the Hennepin County Sheriff's Department and a law student at William Mitchell in the Twin Cities until she was arrested and charged with six Wisconsin bank robberies. It turns out she wasn't pulling heists to make payments on her law school tuition, she was covering her bets at the Mystic Lake Casino, where she had been a regular at the high-stakes blackjack tables. Sue Ellen Schave, twenty-seven, a supervisor of bank tellers at Norwest Bank in Crystal, having dropped one hundred thousand dollars in a single weekend at video poker, negotiated a private line of in-house loans from Norwest. When she was convicted in a federal court, her attorney pushed for a lower sentence, arguing that Ms. Schave is a compulsive gambler. Her crime was the result of an addiction.

It looks as if we have come full circle. In the eighteenth century, indigenous communities in the Minnesota territories—the Dakota and the Ojibwe—were decimated by alcohol consumption. Their vulnerability to that addiction, which still ravages their communities, was exploited by fur traders out to maximize profits. Now the Dakota and the Ojibwe have seized an economic opportunity that offers an escape from a two-hundred-year cycle of addiction and poverty, but that opportunity entails exploiting another addiction. The Indians, to be sure, are not forcing gambling on anyone, any more than the fur traders compelled them to drink. Caveat emptor. The casino advertisements, of course, have a more positive emphasis: "We're changing the hand life's dealt you. Who says you can't change fate?"

The Dakotas seem to be doing just that, at least for themselves. The Prior Lake Reservation, once a landscape of battered trailers and shacks, now looks like an upscale suburb. The reservation is not completely free of the problems of drugs, alcohol, and dysfunctional families—the problems that drove Reverend Cavender into post-traumatic stress disorder—but they have been reduced. There is new self-esteem. Cavender spoke proudly of a new community center that would be completed in the Prior Lake Reservation the next month: four classrooms, a chapel, a courtroom, two libraries, and a community meeting hall. There was a great deal of renewed interest in traditional drumming and chanting. When the community center was finished, he would teach a course in Dakota language in one of the classrooms.

The new wealth, as overwhelming in its way as the old poverty was, is not without its corruptions. In early 1990, casino gambling was virgin territory to the Wisconsin Winnebago. The management, the money, dealing a hand of blackjack—it was all new to them. So a hustler from Chicago showed them how it is done. You know, the basics. Bribes, kickbacks, creative accounting, rewarding friends and punishing enemies. Before long, divisions in the tribe were so deep its government couldn't muster a quorum to conduct council meetings. It came down to a shootout at the Ho-Chunk Casino, tribal members blasting away at each other from behind the slots and cigarette machines. Your standard grade-B Western. That's when the Federal government stepped in. A community can be tested in other ways, however.

"Will the Prior Lake Reservation go the way of many affluent white suburbs," I asked the community's holy man, "trading in tradition for a lifestyle purchased at the Mall of America?"

He acknowledged the dangers, but it was clear that he preferred these challenges to the nuclear winter of rock-bottom indigence. He was willing to roll the dice. Small wonder. Gary Cavender's Prior Lake tribe is far and away the most prosperous in Minnesota. Its Mystic Lake Casino is one of the largest and most successful gambling casinos in the U.S., and from its profits each of the tribe's 150 members receives six hundred thousand dollars per year. That tribe, however, accounts for fewer than one percent of the thirty-one thousand Indians who live on or near reservations in the state. And only ten percent of Mystic Lake's 3,500 employees are Indians. The tribal members themselves, of course, have no economic incentive to seek employment. Seventy percent of the tribe's potential work force is unemployed, the same percentage as before the casino profit sharing. It's just that the unemployed are now very wealthy. The Red Lake Chippewa, by contrast, operate three much less successful casinos in a remote area of the state. Their unemployment rate has actually increased slightly since their casinos opened, from sixty to sixty-four percent. There's no profit sharing and many of the tribe's eight thousand members still struggle with poverty.

The Mille Lacs Chippewa, with their ambitious and successful Grand Casino located much closer to the Twin Cities, have taken a different approach to profit sharing. The lion's share of the proceeds are reinvested in casino expansion and in projects that will benefit the entire Mille Lacs community. They have cut unemployment from forty-five to twenty percent, built schools, and won treaty rights to fishing privileges.

These examples of different tribes raise the question: What effect will the wealth generated by casino gambling have on Indians throughout the state? A handful are becoming millionaires. Some tribes are investing in community building. But there is no discernible effort to scatter the wealth more widely, whether through jump start investments or employment. Those tribes with casinos that cannot boast, as Mystic Lake does, "We're not as big as the Mall of America, but we're close...just 20 minutes away," still experience poverty.

The casinos have created an extreme inequity of wealth in the Indian population that mirrors the nation as a whole. The wealthy few have prospered because they have mastered the capitalist strategies of reinvestment, expansion, and aggressive marketing. The Mdewakanton Dakotas, owners of the Mystic Lake Casino, have recently bought 593 acres for retail and industrial development. In its application to place this land in trust with the U.S. Bureau of Indian Affairs (which would exempt it from property taxes and local zoning laws), the tribe stated, "The Community's intent is to enter areas of the economy unrelated to gaming and entertainment. A strong economy requires diversification." You might say the Mdewakanton Dakotas are simply adhering to the prophetic wisdom of Cloudman, who, despite the vicissitudes of history, was right after all.

"A group of people made the best of what they had, just like Bill Gates and Microsoft," one Prior Lake tribe member was quoted in the papers the other day. "That's basically what's going on here." He conceded, "I sympathize with the other reservations; they do need more economic development." He was poor once himself. No longer. Twenty-seven years old, he owns a nine-hundred-thousand-dollar home and a forty-thousand-dollar Mercedes sports vehicle. He's done what those earliest settlers did after they drove the Dakotas from the land where the Mall of America now stands. He has built an immovable house that announces to the world, "I'm here to stay."

It's a fresh July morning and Doreen Day is brushing out the hair of her daughter Elissa, age six, preparing it for braids.

Elissa will be one of the dancers in a Dakota powwow at Treasure Island Casino. Doreen and Elissa are Ojibwe, but this particular powwow is special for them because it will celebrate the miraculous recovery of a relative, the young daughter of Doreen's sister, who was struck a year ago by a drunk driver, a white man, and was in a coma for four months. Doreen's Ojibwe family came to the powwow last year to ask for the Dakota community's prayers, prayers that in the event were answered. Later today there will be a gift-giving ceremony in which the family will publicly express their gratitude. Elissa is patient under her mother's ministrations, and when her hair is braided she runs off to exchange her Reeboks and denim shorts for moccasins and ceremonial dress.

Doreen is Director of Indian Family Services in Minneapolis. I know her through a mutual friend, Julia Uleberg, who midwifed at Elissa's birth. Doreen often attends powwows with her children, just as her own mother took her back to the reservation for visits and celebrations long after the family moved to St. Paul. Still, a world divides Doreen from her reservation siblings. Alcohol has savaged the lives of many of her kin, as it might have hers if her father had not been murdered one night when he was drunk. She was sixteen at the time and she made a promise to God: she would not drink spirits. "I let that black door stay shut. My father gave me a new life."

Over the past two decades, her family has begun to rebuild itself, to heal. Many families have been decimated by the conditions endemic to native life—poverty, alcohol, displacement. Physical survival alone is problematic; life expectancy among natives is fourteen percent lower than among whites. There are more than twice as many dead Indians in the museums of North America and Europe than there are living in the U.S. The few that become elders, traditional sources of vision to the community, are chronically ill before they are sixty.

Doreen's children go to Indian Survival School where, in addition to learning the skills of white culture, they are taught native history and native values. They apply these values in their critical assessments of the dominant culture that surrounds them. Her children are politically aware, Doreen says; they participate in Earth Day walks and Greenpeace rallies.

I can't help mischievously inquiring about Elissa's Reeboks. Doreen laughs: "She bought them at the Mall of America!"

"Your kids go to the Mall?" I ask incredulously.

"Of course," she says. "They love it."

To them it's a fabulous, almost "untouchable" place, yet they can enter this magical palace any time they choose. They don't go there all the time, but when they go it is always a special occasion, for birthdays or to do Christmas shopping. The little ones go mainly for the special food—the orange chicken at the Panda is Elissa's favorite—and for the Camp Snoopy rides. The older kids are drawn to the clothing stores and the sports shops. For Christmas, they wanted sag shorts and starter jackets and Nikes, and although the family budget has not yet permitted the purchase of a car, Doreen saw that they got the $169 jackets and the $120 Nikes (she bought the shoes on sale—just $79). She even treated herself to extravagant earrings at Macy's (also on discount) to match a blue-green dress she wore on New Year's Eve.

"I haven't worn them since but I loved the indulgence of getting them. They were perfect for that dress."

Her kids love the Mall of America, she tells me, but mall culture isn't their life as it is for many white teenagers. Her kids are centered in Ojibwe culture. She smiles indulgently at their awe before the Mall's glamour.

"But doesn't the Mall represent everything in white culture that is antithetical to Ojibwe tradition?" I ask her. "Its riches are harvested in an economic system that exploits the earth, exhausts its resources, fosters habits of waste, etc., etc."

She is familiar with the clichés.

"Someday they will have to deal with those contradictions," she concedes. "I too have to work in a system that is alien to my values. I make compromises and they will have to. But I am an Ojibwe, and they will be Ojibwe. Of this I am certain."

Our conversation is interrupted by a voice over the loudspeaker announcing the commencement of the Grand Entry. To the accompaniment of drums and chanting, three braves in full regalia—feathers, fringe, bells, and beadwork—move solemnly into a large, rounded space. They are followed by three Vietnam vets in camouflage fatigues, then more braves and more braves and more braves, followed by the women, and then the children, a dancing circle of humanity coiling tighter and tighter. I spot Elissa in her costume of pale blue, pink, and black; across her shoulders, on her waistband, and on her leggings are abstract patterns that suggest oak leaves and eagle feathers. She seems weightless in the deft grace of her movements, like a lovely water bug hovering in the mist above a deep and turbulent river.

Chapter Six

A Village School

THE MALL OF AMERICA'S Leila Anderson Learning Center, a nine-thousand-square-foot facility tucked next to Bloomingdale's, is not, as an experiment in education, unprecedented. Twin Cities students have for some time studied part-time in hospitals, police stations, and businesses. Nor is the learning center the country's first school-in-a-mall, though it is the most ambitious to date. In addition to a high school program, National American University offers several degree programs, and there are adult education classes offered by the University of St. Thomas. But journalists have certainly given the impression that this project is something special: a story in the *New York Times,* an AP story that was carried throughout the country, television crews from as far away as Germany, the Netherlands, Switzerland. To say nothing of ubiquitous quips and references in print and on the airwaves when the school first opened.

The initial outline of course offerings suggested that the Mall school would have a largely liberal curriculum: "Global Connections/Future Studies," "Environmental Issues/Ecology," "Arts in the Marketplace," "Entrepreneurship and Business." These classes would not add up to a full-fledged school with a principal and a school nurse, bells and home rooms, athletic teams and a marching band, pep rallies and proms. The Mall classes and internships would complement traditional classes at existing schools in cooperating districts. One might think that such an opportunity would be broad in its appeal, but at least initially it drew largely disaffected students. For these students, the traditional classroom amounted to a war zone: interminable boredom punctuated by moments of terror. The Mall, by contrast, was a user-friendly environment and there was always the off chance they might learn something useful there. Like how people with money and power run the world.

The first term (February-June 1994) was less ambitious: a single course, "Entrepreneurship and Business," taught by Jerry Cromer-Poire and Mark Loken. For the first month and a half, until the students from Minneapolis schools came on board, there were just sixteen participants and tables were arranged in a big square. The discussions were informal and uninhibited. Once the class swelled to thirty-four, however, the students sat in rows facing the teachers and they stopped talking to each other. They had attended diverse schools in five districts during the morning and then made their way to the Mall by 12:30. On Monday and Tuesday afternoons, they worked at their internships in retail or Mall management; on Wednesdays and Thursdays they came to their classroom.

The classroom did not open directly on the Mall. Far from being a space bombarded by the distractions of shoppers and retail, it resembled a sensory-deprivation box, windowless and white. The fluorescent impersonality was not substantially altered by posters of Michael Jordan, Malcolm X, and Nelson Mandela pinned to the walls.

Jerry, cheerful and rotund and laid back, radiated warmth and generosity. His assistant, Mark, a tall teddy bear of a guy, was also unfailingly respectful of the students. Their style was non-authoritarian; students drifted in and out and some ate their lunch during class. The teachers' pedagogy, on the other hand, was not exactly student-centered. Terms were listed on the board, topics were covered, worksheets filled out. Class attendance was good until May, when it fell off precipitously.

Three years earlier, when they were still pouring concrete at the site of the Mall, representatives of five school districts in the Twin Cities metro area were meeting to lay the foundation for a new kind of school. The recently formed Metropolitan Learning Alliance (Minneapolis, St. Paul, Bloomington, Richfield, St. Louis Park) composed a mission statement for the project: "to prepare a diverse population of learners to function in an increasingly competitive world by creating a non-traditional, innovative, research-based learning environment which utilizes the unique resources of the Mall of America." They articulated what they called "beliefs":

> Education is a preparation for a life of learning and change.
> People learn in a variety of ways.

149

Diversity strengthens us.

People learn by doing.

Learners should participate in developing and implementing their learning experience.

It takes a village to educate an entire person.

Everyone can learn.

This creed has a pedigree older than the nation. When the early immigrants came here, they found a continent that was largely unknown, and it remained so until the nineteenth century, a vast wilderness of new species of plants and animals. Many of the simplest facts of geography were yet to be described. Americans learned about the New World by confronting practical problems in their daily lives; the scholarly tomes and intellectual systems of Europe were of little use to them. Knowledge was not accumulated by an elite few with academic credentials, as it often was in Europe, but by many ordinary people struggling with ordinary lives. The constitution of our new nation would have been inconceivable without the work of philosophers like Rousseau and Locke, but the framers of that constitution, men as different as the patrician Jefferson and the self-made Franklin, shared our native approach to knowledge. By the end of the nineteenth century, a teacher at Harvard, William James, turned this American attitude into a philosophy, put it into a book, and gave it a name: pragmatism.

Americans, of course, did value formal education, indeed believed in it so passionately that they insisted it be available to all and even that it be compulsory. Yet there remained the conviction that learning in the classroom should be related, clearly and repeatedly, to experience in the world. Americans have always seen school as a preparation for material success and participatory democracy. The most influential American educator of this century, John Dewey, emphasized again and again that true knowledge comes not from mere memorization or abstract speculation but from problem solving. Dewey refused to accept a division between the life of thought and the life of action. Education isn't a disinterested exercise of the mind but an introduction to the challenges students will face in the world.

Sounds good, but it's not quite that simple. Nothing is; that is one of the first lessons of education. When he visited this country, Alexis de Tocqueville observed:

> In America the purely practical part of science is admirably understood, and careful attention is paid to the theoretical portion which is immediately requisite to application. On this head the American always displays a clear, free, original, and inventive power of mind. But hardly anyone in the United States devotes himself to the essentially theoretical and abstract portions of human knowledge.... Everyone is in motion, some in quest of power, others of gain. In the midst of this universal tumult, this incessant conflict of jarring interests, this continual striving of men after fortune, where is that calm to be found which is necessary for the deeper combinations of the intellect?

Americans, Tocqueville wrote, "are generally led to attach an excessive value to the rapid bursts and superficial conceptions of the intellect, and on the other hand to undervalue unduly its slower and deeper labors." Yet in the end, Yankee ingenuity depends on these slower and deeper labors. Without Newton and Einstein there is no satellite technology; without a John Von Neumann there are no Apple computers.

There is also another problem. Randolph Bourne, one of John Dewey's most brilliant students, remarked that pragmatism, preoccupied with its problem-solving pursuit of ends, does not adequately weigh the worth of those ends. Caught up in questions of how, it rarely asks why. Values are too often left unexamined.

Anyone who takes this matter of values seriously will no doubt be nonplussed at the thought of a school in a mall, a dismay voiced by David Tilsen, a former Minneapolis school board member who voted against the Mall of America project.

"Isn't that one of our problems, that we have too much commercialism?" he asked. "Isn't there too much emphasis on what kind of tennis shoes you are wearing and what kind of status symbols you have?"

The Mall is designed to keep people moving, not looking at anything too hard for too long; it's the last place anyone would go to think seriously. There is nothing, however, that demands more serious thought.

A recent, much-publicized experiment in education American-style illustrates how a balance of pragmatic learning and reflection on values can be achieved. In 1966 Eliot Wigginton had just finished five years at Cornell. He had an AB in English and an MA in Teaching and he figured he would bring civilization as we know it to the 240-pupil Rabun Gap-Nacoochee

School in Georgia. Rabun Gap was smack in the Appalachians and civilization as they knew it was not civilization as Wigginton knew it. When one of his pupils set fire to his lectern during class, Wigginton conceded there was a difference.

He went home angry and thought of all the ways he could put his students in their place. But he decided to do something else. He walked into class the next day and said, "How would you like to throw away the text and start a magazine?" When the students realized he was serious they allowed as how it was possible. What would the magazine be about? Well, about their community—its people, customs, and values. It would be about civilization as they knew it. So they went out and interviewed kinfolk and neighbors and did research and wrote articles titled "Building a Log Cabin," "Chimney Building," "Rope, Straw, and Feathers Are to Sleep On," "A Quilt Is Something Human," "Churning Your Own Butter," and "Weather Signs." They collected enough donations to put out six hundred copies of their first issue, and when those were sold out they printed six hundred more. They called their magazine *Foxfire,* after a tiny organism that glows in the dark of the local mountains. It wasn't long before folks outside of Rabun Gap, outside of Appalachia, noticed the glow. It got written about in the *Saturday Review,* the *New Republic, National Geographic,* and before long *Foxfire* had subscribers in all fifty states as well as a dozen countries. The students gathered the essays together into a book titled *Foxfire;* it became a national bestseller and inspired a host of similar experiments around the country.

Jerry Cromer-Poire was a young teacher back then. It was the early seventies, the "days of dancing" as he calls them. George Young, then superintendent of the St. Paul school district, launched a learning center for experimental programs with an emphasis on community involvement. The idea was to create structures in which students from different racial and economic backgrounds, highly motivated achievers and kids at risk, could work together in hands-on projects. Jerry, a social-science teacher, teamed up with Steve Trimble, a historian, and thirty students drawn from all the schools in St. Paul, and together they put out a magazine modeled on *Foxfire*. A mix of poetry, recipes, local folkways and mores, *Scattered Seeds* was published once a trimester for five years, eight hundred to one thousand copies of each issue at two to four dollars an issue. Like the *Foxfire* group, they branched out into filmmaking and public service videos. Eventually, however, budget cuts sent them back into the traditional classroom.

Now, six years shy of retirement, Jerry was being given another shot at the dream. This time he was teamed up with Mark Loken, a greenhorn just out of college with one year of teaching experience at a Blackfoot reservation in Heart Butte, Montana. His first day of teaching in Montana, Mark walked into a classroom of "absolute chaos," and behavior didn't improve much as the year wore on and the students got to know him. Their inattentiveness, lack of concentration, and disruptiveness were, in some, the result of fetal alcohol syndrome, but there were economic causes as well. Often the students' parents were unemployed and the students themselves saw no job prospects in a community isolated by distance and welfare. In the nearest town, Browning, half the buildings were boarded up, the fire-gutted movie theater abandoned. The students didn't see much point in struggling to master the knowledge and skills of an alien culture. For Mark it was a tough year.

It's a long way from Heart Butte to the Mall of America, though here too there were students at risk. Half of the thirty-four would-be entrepreneurs in the class were students of color, mostly African-American, a few Asian-Americans. They were not, like the Blackfeet, physically isolated, but the mechanisms of capitalism were, for most of them, as remote as Napoleon's conquest of Europe. As the class stretched on through the spring, these students tended to drift off at their desks, sometimes cradling their heads in their arms.

Once a week, usually on Wednesday, Robert Boone came and talked to them. Robert, as he was called by both teachers and students, was just ending a three-year tenure as the Mall of America's Human Resource Manager. He had put into place the Mall's operating staff and had assisted the first tenants. Now, after years as a corporate soldier at places like Miller Brewing and ITT, he was launching his own entrepreneurial career with a photocopying franchise. An African-American in his early forties, he was the image of success—trim, stylish, articulate, personable, and very bright.

He had grown up in the inner city of Columbus, Ohio— the old Columbus, before urban renewal. Neither of his parents had finished high school; his mother conceived him when she was seventeen. Both his folks worked, his father in construction, then as a bus driver for the Columbus Board of Education, and their combined income never exceeded fifteen thousand dollars. Robert won a basketball scholarship at Central State in Wilberforce but dropped out in the spring of his first year, in 1970. In July he received his invitation to the Vietnam War. "I grew up in the Army."

He started off in Special Services playing at different bases on the Eighth Army basketball team and eventually became a section leader in a helicopter battalion. Twenty years old, he was responsible for twenty-five machines worth a million dollars each, as well as for the personnel who flew and maintained them. He didn't drink and he didn't do drugs and that gave him an edge. He grew comfortable with responsibility and authority. When he came home, he enrolled at Ohio State and graduated with a degree in business.

Robert didn't tell the students this story, nor did he tell them of the special efforts he had made to hire minorities and women when he established the Mall's initial operating staff, placing them in sixty-six percent of the new jobs. Of the first five hundred people he hired, forty percent did not have a checking or savings account and many did not know how to write a check. He didn't recount for the class the lengths to which he went to engage minority businesses, contractors, vendors, suppliers. Perhaps he felt these details were not directly pertinent to the course, though more than three-fourths of the students were minorities and women.

One day the topic was financing a business: leverage, long-term loans, common and preferred stock, retained earnings, cash-flow statements. In reviewing sources of capital

Robert observed that banks usually insist that the business or individual provide a minimum of thirty percent of the cash or capital and dollar-for-dollar liquid collateral. He also noted that getting into a franchise isn't cheap. Twenty years ago, he said, you could start a McDonald's with thirty-five thousand dollars; today it takes $1.2 million. He left unspoken the obvious implications of his example: a young entrepreneur hoping to make his fortune selling hamburgers better begin with four hundred thousand dollars up front and eight hundred thousand dollars in collateral.

During the class break, I chatted with Masai Polk, one of the few students who never drifted off. He was dismayed by what he had just heard.

"Last year I tried to get a credit card at Dayton's. I had to fill out this form they have, and then the lady took it back into their offices—someplace where they check out these forms. I had to wait two-and-a-half hours. Then she told me they couldn't give me the credit card. I guess I didn't have enough collateral."

Yet Masai had been designated, informally, as the one most likely to succeed in this pilot class, the one singled out for visiting journalists to talk to, quoted in the *New York Times,* interviewed by the out-of-town television crews. It was easy to see why. He was handsome, soft-spoken, courteous, serious, ambitious. In his internship in the Mall's marketing department, he came to work in a dark-gray double-breasted suit. Occasionally we would stroll together around the Mall and he would share his gorgeous dreams.

157

"I can see myself as the CEO of my own business," he told me, a statement, oddly, that carried no suggestion of vanity or arrogance. More like a fact of personal history: I was born in Palo Alto, or I hitchhiked to Wyoming one summer when I was seventeen. In Masai's case, the personal history was mostly future tense. His father was an MD in Atlanta and his mother ran a day-care service in Minneapolis. I don't recall learning much more about them than that.

He was, for the moment, stalled between past and future, marking time in his last term at Roosevelt High, "a day-care center run like a prison." In the fall of his junior year, the election of a black homecoming king and a white queen provoked interracial fights that led to wider mayhem and the cancellation of homecoming activities. Students, black and white, from other Minneapolis schools came to Roosevelt to voice their criticism of the racial antagonism, and the media followed up with stories about chronic problems of guns, gangs and drugs.

"They had us by the neck." Masai resented the public shaming and the punitive measures imposed by the principal (which, predictably, did not quell the trouble but made it worse). When the publicity subsided Masai found himself unalterably alienated from his world. In certain moods, "the brothers" became "those clowns."

"That's all they know—negativity. Party, do drugs, join a gang. I don't think like them. If you care about education, you're rejected. They put down the kids with a sense of direction."

At times he sounded more like someone from another generation. "We live in the most irresponsible age of teenagers this world will ever experience."

At school people would tell him, "You don't look happy."

"What's to be happy about? I feel like I've just served four years for a crime I didn't commit."

Next year Masai would enter the University of Minnesota under a program for disadvantaged students, with special counseling, advising, and tutorial resources, resources he intended to make full use of.

"I know the atmosphere is going to be different because it is college." And beyond college? One afternoon Masai led me to Osterman's Jewelers on the West Side, second level. He asked the clerk to take a gold Rolex studded with diamonds from the glass case and, holding it with affection, he invited me to examine it. For what that timepiece cost, you could buy a modest Mercedes Benz.

"Someday," he told me, "I'm going to own this watch."

Unlike Masai, Tameka Miller, another bright, serious student, spoke at length about her family. Her father lives in Chicago, where he works for UPS. Her mother does "assembly" for a company called...Art Tech? Something like that. Tameka was uncertain because the job is unimportant, just a way to pay the bills until her mother completes her course work at a Minneapolis community college. She spoke admiringly of her mother, her "best friend," and her mother's values—education, work, family. Tameka often helps out at home, cooking and looking after her six younger sisters, in addition to holding down part-time jobs. Hers is a close-knit family that often does things together on weekends, watching a movie on the VCR in winter, going to a city park for a picnic when the weather turns warmer. Each summer they travel to Chicago for a week to visit the father.

"My mom and dad have a good relationship. It just didn't work out for them as a couple."

Anticipating college year after next, she planned to head south where it would be cheaper to live. She had extended family in Arkansas, Louisiana, and Mississippi, and she could stay with a relative. On the last day of class she and her friends brought their babies to show them off. Reflecting on her internship at Gigi's, a clothing boutique that targets teenage girls, Tameka spoke of her supervisor with affection and respect. She felt she had learned a lot. Could she see herself as an entrepreneur starting her own business someday? No way. Too complicated, too much to juggle, too many people to deal with. She wanted to be an accountant; she had always done well in accounting classes. As we talked, she fed her seven-month-old son with a bottle.

Masai and Tameka, though of comparable ability, do not have equal prospects for economic success. Tameka is encumbered with family. In class Robert Boone characterized successful entrepreneurs as aggressive, independent risk-takers, driven people who are never satisfied with their achievements and who therefore seldom strike a healthy balance between their business and their personal lives. In launching his new franchise, he said, he was prepared to put in eighty hours a week.

In the opening chapter of the class's textbook, *Applied Economics,* Adam Smith's famous defense of unfettered self-interest is quoted.

> Every individual is continually exerting himself to find the most advantageous employment for whatever capital he can command. It is his own advantage, and not that of society, which he has in mind...but he is in this, as in many other cases, led by an invisible hand to promote an end which was no part of his intention, for the pursuit of his own advantage necessarily leads him to prefer that employment which is most advantageous to society.

The inalienable rights of life, liberty, and the pursuit of happiness seem to have carried the same implication for Americans. "What good I do," Thoreau remarked in *Walden,* "in the common sense of that word, must be aside from my main path, and for the most part wholly unintended." When he visited this country, de Tocqueville used the recently coined term "individualism" to describe this attitude that many have found liberating. It has not worked for everyone, though.

Among people of color, individualism, pushed as hard as Americans push it, has been an alien and even a disabling idea. In *Race Matters,* Cornel West identifies nihilism as the "most basic issue now facing black America."

"This threat is not simply a matter of relative economic deprivation and political powerlessness—though economic well-being and political clout are requisites for meaningful black progress. It is primarily a question of speaking to the profound sense of psychological depression, personal worthlessness, and social despair so widespread in America." Even sympathetic whites, West argues, fail to grasp the real nature of crisis in black communities because "they tend to view people in egotistic and rationalistic terms according to which they are motivated primarily by self-interest and self-preservation." Yet "market forces and market moralities" are a central cause of the present crisis in black leadership. Though a black middle class has grown and prospered in recent decades, that middle class has adopted the prevailing model of the good life as one of "conspicuous consumption and hedonistic indulgence." In effect, the haves have abandoned the have-nots. "One reason quality leadership is on the wane in black America is the gross deterioration of personal, familial, and communal relations among African-Americans. These relations—though always fragile to sustain—constitute a crucial basis for the development of a collective and critical consciousness and a moral commitment to and courageous engagement with causes beyond that of one's self and family."

These are more that just the ruminations of a Princeton philosopher. In *Success Runs in Our Race,* Cleveland entrepreneur George Frazer makes the same point. Calling for a "revival of Afrocentric communal spirit," Frazer argues, "cooperation, collectivism, and sharing are the essential elements. Community is considered before the individual." Frazer has created a national network of more than sixty thousand blacks, what he describes as "a modern version of the Underground Railroad." It is a resource that can be exploited by participants for their own political and economic ends, though

Frazer envisions larger purposes: "While many people think of networks as business tools, they have been used to implement social change." By contrast, he cites the examples of his own city where affluent blacks, like their white counterparts, have fled the urban center for outlying suburbs. The most devastating effect of this flight has been the abandonment of generations of black youth who "have nowhere to go and nothing to do." Frazer quotes the African proverb, "It takes a village to raise a child." He wants to invent a new kind of community, "a new Urban Village."

Interestingly, one of the "beliefs" set down by the Metropolitan Learning Alliance when they were planning the Mall school was a paraphrase of that African proverb: "It takes a village to educate an entire person." It is a notion that has deep American roots. "It is time that villages were universities," Thoreau observes in *Walden*. When I asked Jerry and Mark about this matter of community involvement, each of them replied, "Look around you. The Mall is a community." Taking them at their word, I went out to talk to folks in the community.

Tammy, the manager of Gigi's and Tameka's supervisor in her internship, is twenty-nine. When she was a senior at Eisenhower High in Hopkins, Minnesota, she participated in a program very similar to the one Tameka was in; she attended school half a day and worked in an internship. Had the program made a difference for her? Did she learn anything in her internship she would not have learned just holding down a part-time job? She couldn't say. She couldn't remember anything from the experience. But she has been in retail ever since.

As manager of Gigi's, she was responsible for payroll, personnel, keeping track of daily sales figures, and store maintenance. When it was her turn to clean the bathroom, she cleaned it. She was on her feet all day dealing with teeny-boppers. Her biggest challenge was finding and keeping "sales associates" who would work part-time for minimum wage. Most of those looking for work, she said, come in with a baby in tow and a couple of friends, but without the language skills to fill out an application form. Tammy was on salary, but given the hours she had to put in she was not earning much more than minimum wage herself.

As she approached thirty, she was getting nervous. "I'm getting too old for this work." It's true. The shops at the Mall, with the exception of the anchor stores, are managed and clerked by Generation X. Tammy wanted a job "with a future," something that would give her a living wage and a few medical benefits. Her parents went through the Depression living hand-to-mouth. They had never had much money, but about the time Tammy was born they bought a house for twenty-five thousand dollars on a thirty-year mortgage, an extravagance she expected would forever be beyond her means. Her apartment next to the airport cost her four hundred dollars a month. She couldn't afford to go out on weekends and was usually too exhausted to anyway. When an extra expense, such as dental work, came up, she had to go to her folks for a loan. At some point that would have to stop; her father was retired and in his seventies.

Tammy had considered going to college and getting a degree, but the cost of higher education frightened her. She did not see how she could handle that kind of debt burden. Meanwhile Brauns, Gigi's parent company, had been going through a period of low revenues and management shakeup. Lots of stress all down the line. Regarding Tameka's internship, Tammy did not have a clear idea of what the program's expectations were. Tameka did what the other sales associates did and she had been a conscientious worker. In fact, Tameka would be hired as a part-time sales associate when her internship ended. Tammy would be moving on to a Brauns store in another mall, though she hadn't told her intern this yet.

Tammy was the village that had been teaching Tameka.

Eliot Wigginton and his students at Rabun Gap in Appalachia had a different concept of village. Their *Foxfire* experiment turned out to be, among other things, an on-going course in entrepreneurship and business. Building on the success of their magazine and books, the group bought land in Mountain City, a nearby town of 450, and working in close collaboration with local residents they drew up plans for a regional press, a community historical center, a retail outlet (where only local crafts and products would be sold), a mail-order center, a garden center, a playground and picnic area, an amphitheater, a craft area, and a blacksmith shop. These projects, only a few of which are in place today, were conceived as a form of community renewal. In *Sometimes a Shining Moment: The Foxfire Experiment,* Wigginton lays out the central tenet of his commitment to education: "Every classroom is an act of making citizens, and thus a political act." As he sees it, our national "slogan has always been Land of Opportunity, which, roughly translated, means 'Grab as much as you can,' as opposed to 'Take only what you need.'...What's wrong...is that so many people get stepped on in the process. Individualism makes for competition and division, and that tends to be a very shaky foundation on which to build a society. In such a society, people tend to be so preoccupied with their own concerns that they have little time for those of others or for the greater good." In educating citizens, Wigginton writes, "we should attempt to move students beyond concern with self and self-indulgence as their primary future orientation."

In the entrepreneurship and business class at the Mall, Jerry would often use part of the period to show a news report he had taped from CNN the night before. Sometimes the report had an obvious relevance to the course content, but not always. When Nelson Mandela was sworn in as the new president of a new South Africa, Jerry showed a tape of the inaugural ceremony and emphasized the significance of this moment in world history. There could be no doubt that he was very moved by the occasion. What he did not do was explain to the students how the mechanisms of a market economy had been employed to defend apartheid and to bring it down.

The term the students in the class used in reference to the Mall was not "village" or "community," but "the real world." A classroom in a high school such as Roosevelt in Minneapolis or Central in St. Paul—day-care centers run like prisons, a world of gangs, guns, drugs, and teenage pregnancy—is not the real world, whereas this sanitized neon agora is. The reality of survivors, the future. Teenagers black and white flock to the Mall of America because it seems a space without a history. Terry Baresh, a former director of the Lutheran Social Services Street Program, has said, "Kids need a place to go, and the Mall of America is a neutral territory. It is a place they can go and still remain anonymous. They can be from anywhere. Yet when they are at the Mall, they don't have to be from somewhere."

In the world of the future, you won't have to be from anywhere except the global village, with its global marketplace. Put another way, in a world of franchise cloning, a market is a market is a market. At least that is a lesson the students at the Leila Anderson Learning Center next to Bloomingdale's seem to be absorbing from their hands-on introduction to free-enterprise realities.

Chapter Seven

Generation X and the Way the World Is

At 6:00 P.M. on Labor Day, twenty yellow school buses made their way up 35W to the Mall of America. In them were about 860 entering first-year students of St. Olaf College, a hundred Junior Counselors, and forty faculty members. During their first week at St. Olaf, new students are plunged into a dense schedule of social events designed to introduce them to each other and put them at their ease. This expedition to the Mall, however, was not one of those social events. It represented the "academic component" of Week One, and its purpose was to introduce the students to the idea of a liberal education. Each year a text is chosen to be read and discussed in small groups led by faculty. Two years earlier the common reading was *Antigone;* the preceding year it had been selected *Federalist Papers*. In 1993 it was to be the Mall of America. These days everything is a text.

169

Why did the college (or, more precisely, a committee acting on behalf of the college) choose the Mall of America as an experience that might productively introduce eighteen-year-olds to the virtues of liberal learning? This is a story that requires a digression.

You might say that the visit of St. Olaf's class of '97 to the Mall of America began back in the second decade of this century when a student dropped out shortly after arriving on campus. He wasn't the first or the last student to do so, but he went on to become very famous, and his disdain for the college was recorded, briefly though indelibly, in our national memory. In *The Great Gatsby,* Nick Carraway reports that as a young man Jay Gatsby attended "the small Lutheran college of St. Olaf's in southern Minnesota. He stayed there two weeks, dismayed at its ferocious indifference to the drums of his destiny, to destiny itself, and despising the janitor's work with which he was to pay his way through."

Though I teach at St. Olaf, I have a lot of sympathy with the young Gatsby's frustration. Back when he was here, women were confined to their dorms much of the time; there was no dancing, no card playing, no kissing in dark corners. If you wanted to have a good time, you threw snowballs (in winter) and played baseball (in the spring). You attended chapel under compulsion, you became a nice Ole and married another nice Ole, under compulsion, and went on to live a life of compulsory niceness. Jay was right: better a bullet in the back. Gatsby left St. Olaf not because of low grades and janitorial work but because he saw no connection between what was happening on campus and what happens in "the

170

real world." It wasn't just the Lutheran rectitude; it was all the books and papers that bore no relation, as far as he could tell, to his experience.

We don't talk about Gatsby much at St. Olaf; not from shame, but from a sense of guilt. We failed him. St. Olaf is a school that prides itself on nurturing sound values in its students. "Oles are highly motivated and industrious, moderate to conservative in their political views," reports a recent *Barron's Best Buys in College Education.* "The word 'wholesome' is sometimes used to describe them." Jay Gatsby was, in his own way, highly motivated and industrious when he came to the college. Alas, rebuffed by the institution's indifference to his longings and aspirations, he left before he could be rounded into true wholesomeness.

Now, in the fall of '93, the college was belatedly making amends. We were no longer indifferent to the drums of Gatsby's destiny, to destiny itself. Too much was at stake: national solvency, the future of free-market capitalism, the future of our cities, the future of our ecosystem. John Dewey was right in arguing that education must engage students with the challenges of an ever-changing society. So those of us on the St. Olaf faculty participating in the Mall of America experiment told the class of 1997 about Gatsby and pragmatism and the pitfalls of the unexamined life. We gave them two sheets of questions of the kind a contemporary Socrates might raise, we told them they were forbidden to make purchases, we loaded them into a wagon train of school buses, and we headed north to America's largest shopping mall.

171

The visit was relatively trouble free. There was a bit of a ruckus around 8:30 P.M. when a group broke into a rousing repertoire of dorm songs on the second level of the rotunda. Five security officers raced to the site brandishing badges and walkie-talkies and accused the students of committing an unauthorized public performance. Fortunately an assistant dean was on hand to mediate the crisis. Otherwise, students drifted about sharing impressions and occasionally conducting an impromptu interview—with a clerk at Victoria's Secret, with a waitress at Hooters. Some of the guys shot baskets at Oshman's.

———

We gathered our students and got them home by ten, and the next evening faculty met with them in small groups to explore the experience. I sat in on two discussions and led two myself. Later, when I ran into colleagues, I asked how their conversations had fared. The consensus seemed to be that the results were mixed. Each group had met for an hour. Some were lively and others sedate, but most students contributed. The real measure of success for the faculty, though, was the degree to which the students grappled with what we considered the "deeper" questions—the sorts of questions we gave them before they went. When I asked one group at the beginning of our discussion what they thought our reason was for taking them to the Mall, they responded with facetious answers: it's cheaper than theater, it got them off campus, it was a bonding experience. Then one guy, a farm boy as it turned out, said, "Oh, you mean the reasons you'd give our parents for taking us there." So they gave me answers closer to what they sensed I wanted: the Mall poses questions about America's future, it's a familiar experience we haven't examined very carefully, etc. Early on I was reminded that though eighteen-year-olds may be naive about a lot of things, there are some matters about which they are not: malls and education are two of these. But because *Barron's* is right, that St. Olaf students are by and large wholesome people, they were kind and played along.

They noted right away that it was weird to be in a mall and not be able to shop. "Oh, but we were shopping," one girl remarked. "You mean window-shopping?" someone asked. "No," she replied. "We were shopping." The others paused for a moment and then seemed to take in the Zen epiphany, though it slipped through my grasp.

Many observed, however, that when you can't actually buy something in a mall, time slows and lengthens. They noticed many of the tricks the Mall plays with your mind: behind every experience is a calculation. Did this manipulation disturb them? Not really. These tricks are why people go to malls—why they go to movies and rock concerts, why they watch television. Politics, school—manipulation is the weather we breathe. This wasn't cynicism; it was a frank observation. I had asked for a frank discussion of the subject, hadn't I?

The students commented on how comfortable the shoppers seemed. Sometimes you could see them doing private things in public places: they were out and about but they hadn't really left home. The mall is safe the way home is safe, but for a different reason. It is elaborately controlled, though the controls are mostly out of sight and out of mind, which is nice because then you don't feel controlled. In fact, you feel quite free, comfortable with your impulses. Not like in a real city, with all the filth, the homeless, the constant possibility of violence. As cities get further and further out of control, this contrast sharpens.

Some discussion groups explored ways in which the Mall of America is like and not like a city. It has streets and districts (South Avenue, Upper East Side), it has a park (Camp Snoopy), it has police, postal and banking facilities, restaurants, entertainment—and shops, of course. It doesn't have theaters (unless you count the "theaters" in Camp Snoopy), it doesn't have concert halls (though full and chamber orchestras regularly perform in the Mall), it doesn't have a sports arena (though athletic contests are sometimes held in the rotunda), it doesn't have a library (though it does have bookstores). There are fourteen movie screens but no condos or apartments. There is a clinic with four doctors and a dentist but no hospital. The biggest difference, the students decided, is that cities bring people together for all kinds of reasons, but people come to malls simply to shop and have fun.

Is it only people with money to spend who come to malls? Not at all, one girl responded, malls are a boon to the less educated and less affluent. It's cheap entertainment. They probably can't buy anything in Bloomingdale's, but there is always Sears or Filene's Basement or, if they are really strapped, Buck Boutique and Everything's $1.00. What about the poor in less industrialized parts of the world, I pursued: in Asia, Africa, and Latin America? Is the wealth of free market capitalism within their grasp? Can you imagine a future in which mega-malls cover the globe? Can the earth sustain an exponentially multiplying human population in the style we Americans have grown accustomed to?

An abashed pause greeted this challenge. The question was hardly unfamiliar to these students, but they had no answer and, more disturbingly, they doubted that anyone had an answer. A few tried an outflanking maneuver: post-colonial societies would not abandon their traditions, customs, and values. The power of tribal memory is very strong; look at Iran.

Ah, but does tribal integrity have a viable future: look at the former Yugoslavia. Given enough time, given the material rewards, why wouldn't others do as we have done, adjust tradition to the requirements of a competitive market? We seem to live quite happily with the contradiction between conspicuous consumption and the Christian gospel. Islam seems to be an ideology opposed to Western-style capitalism, but Mohammed was a businessman before he became the Prophet and he was never an enemy of competitive commerce. The steady pounding of rock music around the world has already softened the defensive position of the last holdouts. In remote jungles, last year's hits are playing. Levi's and Coke, MTV and cable, are establishing beachheads in the most forbidding terrain. And behind them: megamalls?

Silence.

We segued back to easier topics. The appeal the Mall makes to each of our senses. Its state-of-the-art recycling facilities. The hour drew to a close and the students departed to the next event on their heavily-scheduled Week One agenda.

Issues raised by that mall visit resurfaced in one of my classes in the first week of the semester. I usually begin my survey of modern British literature with a play by George Bernard Shaw, and this time it was *Major Barbara,* the most devilishly paradoxical of Shaw's dramatic works. In fact, the character of the title, Barbara, is offered a devil's contract by her father.

Andrew Undershaft is a prosperous weapons manufacturer who sells his lethal innovations to anyone who has the money to buy them. His personal motto: "Unashamed." His daughter is a major in the Salvation Army until he demonstrates to her that her charitable organization serves his purposes, not God's. By alleviating the sharpest miseries of the underclass and directing their thoughts to heaven, the Salvation Army "draws their teeth" and provides an "invaluable safeguard against revolution." He pays for this service with generous donations. "All religious organizations exist by selling themselves to the rich." When Barbara sees that her soup kitchen is in fact supported by her father's blood-tainted money, she resigns in despair.

Her father is not an unkind man, however, and he offers an alternative to despair. He invites Barbara and her fiancé, a professor of Greek named Adolphus Cusins, to assume control of the Undershaft munitions business. He takes them to the company town, which turns out to be a little utopia, a corporate culture very like that of contemporary Japanese corporations. Give people work and a decent wage, Undershaft tells his daughter, before you talk to them of the Kingdom of God. Without bread there is no morality. "Poverty blights whole cities; spreads horrible pestilences; strikes dead the very souls of all who come within sight, sound, or smell of it." Robust free-market capitalism, not gospel meekness, is what the dispossessed of the earth require. "You have made for yourself something that you call a morality or religion or whatnot. It does not fit the facts. Well, scrap it. Scrap it and get one that does fit."

There is, of course, the nasty paradox that the work and wages of Undershaft employees require that elsewhere others are blown to pieces. No war, no profits. Undershaft forecloses any facile solution to this dilemma. He tells Barbara and Cusins that if they assume the management of the business, they must bind themselves to one fundamental rule: "To give arms to all men who offer an honest price for them, without respect of persons or principles: to aristocrat and republican, to Nihilist and Tzar, to Capitalist and Socialist, to Protestant and Catholic, to burglar and policeman, to black man, white man, and yellow man, to all sorts and conditions, all nations, all faiths, all follies, all causes, and all crimes." In addition, Adolphus Cusins must change his name and become Andrew Undershaft. Become Andrew Undershaft? The older man warns the younger, once you accept this power and assume control, "You will never again do as you please." This business, he warns, has a will of its own. Yet he baits the scholar with this appeal: "Plato says, my friend, that society cannot be saved until either the Professors of Greek take to making gunpowder, or else the makers of gunpowder become Professors of Greek."

This raw summary doesn't begin to do justice to the wit and verve of Undershaft's negotiations with Barbara and Cusins. In the end the father carries the day. He persuades the next generation to confirm his power by taking it from him.

"You cannot have power for good," Cusins concedes, "without having power for evil too."

Barbara agrees: "Turning our backs on...Undershaft is turning our backs on life."

"Then the way of life lies through the factory of death?" Cusins asks his bride-to-be.

"Yes, indeed," she replies.

There followed in our classroom a lively give-and-take, an exploring of paradoxes, agreements to disagree. At the end of two days of discussion, I took a straw vote: three-fourths of the class felt Barbara and Cusins could make a significant difference in the system.

I opened the next class with a request. "I would like you to write an in-class response to this question: 'What scope do individuals or nations have to pursue their own purposes through a competitive global economy? Or, has free market capitalism become so powerful that it conditions and shapes the purposes of individuals and nations?' I want a ten-minute gut-reaction," I said to the students. "These won't be graded; in fact you don't need to put your name down if you don't want to."

In contrast to the earlier vote, two-thirds of these response papers conceded, often reluctantly, that Emersonian faith in self-determination must be scaled down radically. There were a minority of optimists, one of whom wrote, "Capitalism is

not a natural law and thus it is a human invention.... Therefore, I believe that it is possible for an individual or nation to
have an impact and change the way we view it today." The
pessimists, however, took this argument in a very different
direction: "Generally, the individuals within the society choose
to introduce capitalism into their society or country, as in the
Czech Republic. However, once this is done, the free market
seems to take on a life of its own." The free market is never
really free (for example, beyond government controls), many
students pointed out, but nevertheless it is freer than we are.

"B. F. Skinner once said we may have created society, but
we are controlled by our own creation." Most telling of all
was this analogy: "This is a Babel whose language is a silent
language—that of currency, and whose structure is an invisible one. It proceeds from us but it is greater than any of us,
and greater than all of us. Immensely so."

What then is the point of a liberal education if it does not
really liberate? "If I did not believe it was possible to shape
the world I live in," wrote one student, "I would not be in
this college." Another saw this matter differently. "As a student I am already part of capitalism and although I am learning to despise capitalism, especially its effects on the world, I
am going to graduate and have to live devoted full-time to
capitalism in order to have money to eat/live. The whole business is a wave, we are riding it until it crashes and then what?"

Yet another student put the dilemma this way: "My gut
tells me free market capitalism has overtaken us, but my intellect tries to fight it with every step and I'm ashamed to admit

it, because my intellect is losing and it makes me not want to reveal my name."

Many students felt that it comes down to a matter of will rather than understanding. "So the question of whether people have the power to change the free-market capitalist system is rendered moot by the observation that even if they had the power, most people would never use it." More simply, "We need money to live and breathe."

In *The Great Gatsby,* Nick tells us, "the truth was that Jay Gatsby of West Egg, Long Island, sprang from his Platonic conception of himself. He was a son of God—a phrase which, if it means anything, means just that—and he must be about his Father's business, the service of a vast, vulgar and meretricious beauty...and to his conception he remained faithful to the end." Unwilling to examine his values, he was destroyed by them.

It would be a shame if that happened to us.

Chapter Eight

Frankenstein, the Inner Child

W HEN I FIRST LEARNED that the Mall of America would include an "Imagination Center," I couldn't imagine what it would be. The problem was that word "center." I've always thought creativity and inspiration, those powers of the imagination, are like the Holy Spirit: invisible, unpredictable, forever on the move. Could they be nailed down to a center?

So as soon as the Mall opened, I headed straight for the Imagination Center on South Avenue (as straight as one can head in the Mall) and discovered the whole thing will be built out of Legos. I say "will," because the Imagination Center is, by design, always still under construction, plastic pillars and girders rising up three stories, but with no upper floors and no ceilings. Even the construction workers are made of Legos; they wear hard hats and are perched everywhere. On ground level there is a Lego factory turning out giant Lego bricks on a conveyor belt. It has glowing pipes and knobs, a

TV monitor spinning a kaleidoscope of refracting possibilities, a crazy clock, its hands whirling way too fast. This clock isn't really speeding up the completion of the Imagination Center but just the opposite: pushing everything at light speed into the past.

Huge dinosaurs are prowling around. (Will someone please stop that crazy clock?) There is a red tyrannosaur that must be twenty feet tall, and its jaws open and close. There is a blue and gray iguanodon; a gray, brown-backed triceratops; a yellow and green pachycephalosaur; a red and gray stegosaur. Some of these critters are big. Brachiosaur, with its yellow throat and belly, looks twenty-five feet long. These lizards (all of them made out of Legos) have eyes that glow and parts that move, and some of them have young ones. The babies of maiasaur ("good mother reptile") are busting out of their eggs. One little fellow (little for a maiasaur) is poking up out of its shell, and there's a shell standing on two small legs, turning this way and that in confusion. A pterodactyl hovers overhead, protecting her nest of newborn, their beaks wide open and ravenous. In the middle of the Imagination Center is a reptile—fifteen feet long, ten feet high?—that you won't find in dinosaur books in the library. He's got yellow roller skates with blue wheels on his feet and he's wearing red-white-and-blue exercise pants held up by red suspenders. He carries a boom box and wears headphones. Everything built from Legos. What kind of dude is this? Rockosaurus? Raposaurus? Stretched out on the carpet is a big gray dinosaur speckled with red, yellow, black, white, and blue Legos, dozing lazily like a family dog. Kids can't resist bringing Legos and adding warts, zits, and beauty spots.

These dinosaurs, big as they are, don't have the whole place to themselves. A three-ring circus is in full swing—a cyclist peddles on a high wire overhead, his assistant suspended underneath; trapeze artists soar through the air; an acrobatic team of six brothers is performing, one of them poised in midleap; another spins plates balanced on poles. An animal trainer in a cage, surrounded by big cats, compels a tiger to jump through a glowing hoop. Clowns dressed in striped and baggy pants are dousing birthday candles in a bakery shop with hoses attached to a nineteenth-century pump wagon. Little black dogs yap around their feet. The top-hatted ringmaster straddles a big drum.

And way, way up, three stories up (will there ever be a ceiling on this thing?) the space station Freedom and two astronauts float in space. Beyond them is a space station of the future with more astronauts conducting dazzling experiments. Look at those lit-up spirals! Wait a minute. Isn't that the Red Baron up there as well? Good grief, Charlie Brown—this place is out of control! Someone run and tell Willie Wonka the factory is going berserk. And will someone pleeese stop that crazy clock?!

Adults are walking around saying things like "Oh, my," and "Gosh," and "Wow." Occasionally you hear a kid's voice, "Right here, Dad, behind you." Almost all the children, and there are tons of them, are on the carpeted floor building fantastical models with heaps of Lego bricks and plastic parts. Three-year-olds, teenagers—even their dads, for Pete's sake—

are bent over putting together and pulling apart. Some are sprawled right on the carpet, some are sitting around plastic work tables held six inches above the ground by Lego guys in hard hats, and some are seated around plastic picnic tables spilling over with Legos. Kids and kids and kids, buzzing and humming, humming and buzzing. It's enough to make the Cat in the Hat cry out for law and order.

Will someone pleeeeese stop that crazy clock?!

The sales clerks are mostly young people themselves, wearing hard hats (they'd better!) and elaborate name tags made out of Legos. I ask Emily why she picked her particular pin and she looks at me strangely. She made it herself. Am I lost? Don't I know where I am? This is the Lego Imagination Center. You make your own stuff here.

"Gosh."

"Oh, my."

"Right here, Dad, behind you."

I look up at the Lego construction workers perched on beams and platforms overhead doing their darnedest to bring this project to completion. Good luck, guys.

Lego is more than a toy company. It's a philosophy of life, or at least a theory about children. The company has published several books on play and creativity, and it even has an in-house philosopher, Olaf Damm, whose job it is to pursue these themes. The key to Lego's success, as Olaf sees it, is the nature of children.

"Children need to be active. You will never see passive children. A healthy child is always looking for something interesting to do.... They find out and investigate. They want to use their own resources."

The possibilities in most toys are quickly exhausted, often within two weeks after Christmas. And no single toy could ever be inexhaustible in its potential, though a toy system might be. From the time it perfected its basic brick, Lego (in Latin, the word means "I put together") has challenged children not to follow instructions or to recreate company models but to come up with fresh inventions. To honor those who accept the challenge, Lego publishes photographs of models created by children.

Kids are always outdoing each other. A spaceship that is part machine and part dragon. A two-foot-tall robot chews spaghetti, digests it, and ejects bits of pasta, eyes flashing with pleasure; it can also walk, turn, and carry objects in its hands. The British have a Lego Club magazine, *Bricks 'n' Pieces*, that sponsors a contest each year. Sometimes the challenge is to do much with little. In 1982 the Lego company invited children to enter designs in a competition restricted to models with fifteen or fewer pieces. There were five thousand entries, including a ten-year-old's balloon-driven car.

"Play is very important," says Olaf Damm, "because in play children use their senses, their brains, imagination, social ability—all kinds of resources are activated in the play process. Play is for the most part undisciplined, free, voluntary, and it's fun, and we should never forget that."

Everybody loves to play, of course, not just children. The Minnesota Chapter of the American Institute of Architects stages an annual Lego contest in the Mall's rotunda. The theme varies from year to year—the zaniest skyway, the zaniest skyscraper—and teams representing local firms gather on a Saturday afternoon in October to assemble fantastical structures out of Legos. These creations have to be built on the spot in an intense four-hour competition. Sixteen teams registered for the 1997 competition, teams representing huge firms with international clients and teams from modest partnerships. Each worked feverishly to put together the zaniest skyscraper and, at the end of the four hours, the dazzling results of their efforts ranged in style from space age to Frank Gehry to Dr. Seuss. When the first prize was announced, the winners shrieked and cheered uninhibitedly.

In *The World of Lego Toys,* there is a full-page photograph of a New Guinean father in a remote settlement wearing a bone through his nostrils and a headdress. He is seated cross-legged on a mat, absorbed in assembling a model with Legos from a set brought to his village by a Danish traveler. In the text we are told the "man and his children ignored the pictures on the box and designed their own towers and animal figures on wheels." Without this play of mind and hand, there is no art, no science, no religion, no culture that is recognizably human.

Ten months after the Mall's opening, the Minneapolis Crisis Nursery, a resource for abused children, sponsored an event titled "The Great Create" in the Metrodome. On a sunny Saturday in June when the Twins were playing out-of-town, they heaped more than a million Lego and Duplo bricks on the playing field and invited the general public in with the slogan, "Do Something Constructive." There was a rock band, clowns, face-painting, a silent auction of Lego sculptures by local heroes and national celebrities. The million-plus plastic parts strewn over the electric green Astroturf glittered like the inexhaustible treasure of a fairy-tale emperor. Parents and kids were similarly heaped all about. The stands were empty: no spectators, only players.

In the middle a huge black gorilla was being constructed out of Duplo bricks by Model Designer Paul Chrzan and Master Builder Mike Reis, both in their early twenties. The gorilla, an impressive replica of the real thing hunched over on his forearms gorilla-fashion, was six feet; erect, he would be twice that. Mike and Paul had been working on him for twenty-nine hours and he was all but completed. When I asked Mike what qualities the Lego company looked for in selecting master builders, he said, "Enthusiasm," and Paul added that enthusiasm is the most important qualification for a model designer as well.

"It helps to have played with Legos as a kid." Then he observed with a smile, "But that's just about everyone."

He was trained as a sculptor, though he worked as a baker before joining Lego. He had designed some of the installations in the Mall's Lego Imagination Center—the space station Freedom, some of the circus acrobats, the animal trainer and the big cats, the blimp.

There are five Lego model designers, he told those of us gathered around his gorilla, who work in Canada, the U.S., and Latin America, plus two or three master builders for each designer (designers create and builders execute). Paul estimated that there may be as many as thirty designers in Europe, mostly in Denmark, though their territory also includes Asia, Australia, and Africa.

When the man next to me asked, "What do you think about Flexiblocks?" Mike and Paul stopped smiling and replied, "They're okay. We prefer Legos, of course." They went back to work, but I was curious and asked the man, "What are Flexiblocks?"

"They're just like Legos," he said, "but they snap together at the ends so that they're hinged. They have another dimension. Better than Legos, definitely. You can do a lot more with them."

He gave me his business card: Abi Assadi, AEC Engineering. He was a structural engineer and his wife had just launched a company to produce and market educational products, Intelligent Ideas. I couldn't quite visualize these Flexiblocks, but I guessed he knew what he was talking about.

"How come I haven't heard of them?" I asked.

"They've only been out a year or so and haven't broken into commercial retail yet. The big chains are too cozy with Lego, which naturally wants to shut them out of the market. It won't work. Flexiblocks are going to be very big. Better product."

"Does anybody sell these Flexiblocks now?"

"The Science Museum," he told me. "Places like that. But not for long. They're going to take off."

Lego was attempting to muscle out an innovative competitor? Not Lego. If ever there was a company open to new possibilities, committed to innovation, it is Lego. I suspected Abi Assadi might have a Middle Eastern prejudice against superpowers, a conspiracy theory about the struggles of small operations. Still, I thought I should check out Flexiblocks for myself.

When I left "The Great Create," I headed to the Science Museum and bought a starter set. I asked the clerk how they were selling. It's hard to keep them stocked, she told me. Kids love them. When I got home, I opened my box and saw what Abi was talking about: the hinged design. It did open up new possibilities, but after an hour of playing with them I decided Abi had overestimated their threat to Lego's market share. They would make it into mainstream retail, no question, and turn a healthy profit, but pull the rug out from under Lego?

If Lego goes under, it will be because of more ominous competition: interactive technology. The Nintendo Company earns more after-tax profits each year than all U.S. movie studios combined. CD-ROMs offer three-dimensional action dramas with no set plot line and "complete viewer control," like George Lucas's *Indiana Jones and the Fate of Atlantis,* with forty computer characters, eight thousand spoken lines, and all sorts of possible outcomes. Television and news reports tell us almost daily that affordable, user-friendly virtual reality is just around the corner. Lego will survive Flexiblocks, but digitized fantasy plugged into every home by the phone company is something else entirely. The future will be built out of bytes, not bricks, as the Lego Company well knows. In the eighties, they went to MIT and collaborated with education and computer specialists to design a pilot program for Hennigan School, a public school in Boston where computers can be plugged into Lego possibilities. Children are able to design sci-fi creatures such as "Walker," a prototype of a model powered by vibrations. Will innovations like these enable the company to keep up with the postmodern technological juggernaut? Maybe those Lego dinosaurs in the Imagination Center are ironic symbols of the company in an age when toys, especially interactive toys, fight to the death over territory. According to an executive of the Intel Corporation, "These are going to be the range wars of the twenty-first century and not everyone is going to survive." In the twenty-first century, perhaps my son will have to take his children to the Science Museum to show them Lego technology.

Hans Moravec, Director of the Mobile Robot Laboratory of Carnegie Mellon University, envisions in his book *Mind Children* a day when thinking machines of human invention will stride across a world stage and even "threaten our existence because they are alternative inhabitants of our ecological niche." Actually, the earth, in Moravec's view, is far too humble a theater for these actors. "These new creations, quite unlike the machines we know, will explode into the universe, leaving us behind in a cloud of dust."

Predicting the future of technology, though, is tricky business. Take the prediction that human beings will someday fly. That would seem to be a genuine prediction that was accurate; any number of people claimed it would happen before it did. The prediction, however, isn't very impressive. For one thing, these early forecasts didn't envision anything radically new, but just fiddled with the familiar: bird + man = birdman. This is like science fiction that conjures up extraterrestrial creatures from another galaxy. Usually they have bilateral anatomies, as we do; on a stretch they might have radial anatomies, like starfish. Where are the extraterrestrials in six spatial dimensions? The first problem with crazy predictions is that they are not crazy enough.

Leonardo da Vinci is a good illustration of this dilemma. In his notebooks, we find innumerable predictions of human flight. This was more than whimsy with Leonardo; we could say he was dead serious about the possibility if it weren't for the fact that he dealt with it so playfully. And he isn't vague. He doesn't just say that someday we'll fly, he attempts to describe how flight will be realized. A lot of his mock-ups are of the usual sort, rearrangements of familiar variables. Leonardo's imagination was governed by two analogies, both wrong: human flight will mime bird flight, and bird flight is like swimming under water. His arguments in support of these premises sound good, but anatomical problems ranging from metabolism to centers of gravity (most of them anticipated by Leonardo) make muscle-powered flight for humans impractical. His proposed solutions can be grotesquely comical— the head and neck harnessed for directional control, the feet in stirrups connected by ropes and pulleys to the wings. In one design, the legs, when straightened, make the downstroke, while the hands accomplish the upstroke.

In the hodge-podge of unworkable ideas, however, is one that has nothing to do with birds or swimming: it's the first prototype of the screw helicopter. Leonardo's full helix would be less efficient than separate rotor blades, but here is an inspiration that might have taken off. His description suggests that he may have tested a small model.

This is a glimpse of the future that is very close to the mark and it is suggestive in several respects. First, this contraption, inspired by a child's spinning top, would have seemed to Leonardo's contemporaries his most fanciful, least likely hypothesis, while for us (with our twenty-twenty hindsight) it is his most promising intuition. Second, it is not a prediction but an inventor's model, a conception that is interesting and valuable because it is specific rather than general. Leonardo wasn't prophesying a helicopter, he was drafting one—almost. What he needed was more power than human muscle can provide, power that would eventually be generated by yet another invention, the internal combustion engine. That's the third notable feature of Leonardo's prototype: a successful helicopter entails multiple innovations. Because advances in engineering are seldom linear and discrete, prediction of a non-trivial development requires foreseeing not one event but many. Check out the 1955 issue of *Scientific American* devoted to automation and browse through the contributions of specialists writing before the advent of silicon chips and superconductors.

Which is not to say that we shouldn't listen to specialists who make predictions about the future of their fields. Engineers, no less than artists, have their visions. We should just bear in mind that their craziest ideas are probably not crazy enough.

When Hans Moravec looks into the future, he sees a self-replicating robot that

> would be a marvel of surrealism to behold. Despite its structural resemblance to many living things, it would

be unlike anything yet seen on earth. Its great intelligence, superb coordination, astronomical speed, and enormous sensitivity to its environment would enable it to constantly do something surprising, at the same time maintaining a perpetual gracefulness.

Right now children at MIT are locked into computers, mocking up a new generation of Lego possibilities. To say nothing of post-Lego possibilities. In *The Media Lab: Inventing the Future at MIT,* Stewart Brand describes a project called Vivarium. "Mission: create 'life.' Enable school kids to invent and then unleash realistic organisms in whole 'living' computerized ecologies—learn about the universe's creation by doing some of their own. The animals they create would behave, learn, even evolve independently." The technical innovations necessary for all this have not yet come into being and the project's founder, Alan Kay, gives it "only medium chances of success." In other words, Vivarium is about where the helicopter was in Leonardo's notebook.

As far as Hans Moravec is concerned, these fantasies don't go far enough.

[All] such fabrications are limited by the imaginations of their human creators. Our increasingly complex systems are capable of creating their own surprises, and in times to come we can expect shockingly original gremlins to arise spontaneously in our intelligent machinery, the result of unexpected interactions or mutations of existing parts. A few stirrings have already been observed.

But do we really want a self-replicating mutant hacker monkeying around with the world banking system or the Strategic Air Command? Not to worry; natural selection will preserve a precarious order. "Our best-laid plans are thus foiled, but conversely our descendants are spared the consequences of the limits in our vision. Our intelligence can control the future only imperfectly, and only in the near term."

For instance, imagine this scenario: You are a thirty-something housewife living in the next millennium. A millennium is a fairly broad time frame, so let's focus on one day, a difficult day. You are sitting at your kitchen table. You haven't eaten a bit of breakfast and you hope the kids had all their stuff together when they ran to the school bus because you can't remember a thing they were wearing. The same sentences keep appearing in your mind, like puzzling commands on the screen of your word processor. You read them and think about them, but when you push what you think are the right keys, the same commands keep coming back. They are sentences in a letter you got from the bishop of your diocese yesterday. The letter, typed on his secretary's computer, told you and all the other parishioners that your priest of the last fifteen years had not really been a priest at all—he hadn't even been human.

Father Brannigan, when he was not yet Father Brannigan, had sprung from the head of ZEUS, a super-secret research and development lab of the Army. He was one of twenty prototypes of the New Soldier, eight-million-dollar men who could take anything the enemy dished out and give back worse. Because these would be agents who might be called on to work alone—in guerrilla forays or in espionage—they were programmed with a fair amount of independence of thought and an extraordinary savvy in reading the minds of interrogators. The intelligence of each model (Code name RAMBO 1, 2, 3...) was programmed slightly differently to create controlled variables in the experiment. Rambo 2 was dropped into Honduras and was never heard from again. Special Forces combed the jungles for clues, satellites scanned every inch of Central America with infrared sensors calibrated to unique trace metals in the AWOL machine, but nothing turned up. The Army stopped the full-press search after reporters began sniffing around the operation.

Some weeks later, a young man calling himself Ted Brannigan walked into Thomas Aquinas Church in Miami and announced to a priest that he wished to enter the seminary. He was completely without surviving family, he told the bishop to whom he was sent, and without close friends, for that matter.

"Yet I have never been closer to God," he told the prelate. The Church subjected Mr. Brannigan to a battery of psychological tests, tests he passed with flying colors. In his letter to the seminary on Brannigan's behalf, the bishop wrote, "Never in my thirty years in the Church have I met a man so supremely qualified for a life of service in Christ. Would that he were ordained and at work in my diocese right now."

Father Brannigan did not return to the bishop's diocese, but went north to serve in your church. You can remember the first day he introduced himself to you—the firm handshake, the grin. You left thinking, God, a sexy priest. You were half in love with him already and would stay half in love with him. He married you to somebody else, and you asked him to baptize your children and give last rites to your father. When there were troubles in the marriage, he was the one you turned to, to confess, to seek help...and love. There were minor things, they seemed major at the time, laughable now. And then there were awful things, infidelity and an abortion, things you had no right to take to a priest, but you did because you knew you could.

And yesterday you learned that the priest who forgave you wasn't a priest at all; he was a machine programmed to read minds. It was as if God had pushed a giant number-two pencil down from the sky and started to erase your whole life.

Is it afternoon already? The kids will be home soon. You better begin to make yourself presentable. The doorbell rings...a salesman? Just what you need.... It's a special delivery letter; you sign for it...and the handwriting catches you. You tear the envelope open and inside is a letter to you from Father Brannigan. Not a letter to the parish, not a letter turned out on a computer, but a handwritten, personal letter to you.

Dear Jill,

By now you've gotten the bishop's letter telling you all about me—well, not all. But what he says is true. I am not what I appeared to be...that is what they tell me. I am surrounded by angry people, most of them wearing clerical collars, and soon I will be surrounded by angry people in uniform. I will never again see you or anyone else in the parish, and I thought I ought to write to someone, not to defend myself, but to ask for forgiveness. I'm writing to you because you, more than anyone I've known, are capable of love.

Why did I become a priest? I honestly don't know. Why does anyone become a priest? This will sound crazy under the circumstances, but I think I became a priest because I came to believe that that was what I was created to do. I can't explain it...I don't want to explain it. But I don't want you to doubt that the grace of God you experienced through me is anything less than the grace of God. Is that so hard to believe? Is it impossible for the Maker of heaven and earth to take a piece of machinery and make it an instrument of love? You can no more deny God that power than you can deny the power of your own love inside you now.

They say that all I've done is null and void—well, some of them do. Others aren't sure. I guess I've created a whole new set of theological and ethical questions that will keep the seminaries occupied for years. Not to mention the political problems. If I could laugh, I would laugh. If I could cry, I would cry.

I can't do either, as you now know. I'm counting on you to love me because I cannot love myself and I'm asking you to keep faith in all those blessings that came to you when you were in my care. What does Paul say? "Now there are varieties of gifts, but the same Spirit; and there are varieties of service, but the same Lord; and there are varieties of working, but it is the same God who inspires them all in every one."

Peace,

Father Brannigan

We think of *Frankenstein* as a parable of the dangerous excesses of science, but early in the novel Mary Shelley's protagonist tells the reader that his aspirations to godlike knowledge and power began in childhood. "The world was to me a secret which I desired to divine," he reports. "Curiosity, earnest research to learn the hidden laws of nature, gladness akin to rapture as they were unfolded to me, are among the earliest sensations I can remember." Not every child is destined to become a scientist, but inside most children there is a Frankenstein of some kind. One sees it in the enthusiasm with which they master software that baffles their parents.

There are little Frankensteins all over the Mall of America. I was shopping at FAO Schwarz (W 122) when I overheard a conversation between a father and his son. The boy was asking about the FBI and the CIA. At first he wanted to know how they were different and then he wanted to know pretty much everything. He was about seven, that age when each answer provokes a dozen new questions. This curiosity is a wonderful quality in children, but every parent knows there are times when enough is enough, and that afternoon his father finally reached the limit of his patience.

"Okay," he told the boy, "now I have a question for you. What question does a person ask after he's asked every question in the universe?"

The son looked at the father and said, "Have I missed anything?"

Chapter Nine

The Whirlwind

"This weather seems to be holding back something that it might let loose any minute. If I were a wild animal, I'd hunt my hole and dig it plenty deep. If I were a wild goose, I'd spread my wings and get out of here."
—Pa, in Laura Ingalls Wilder's *The Long Winter*

Where were you when I laid the foundation of the earth? Tell me, if you have understanding....
Have you entered the storehouses of the snow, or have you seen the storehouses of the hail,
Which I have reserved for the time of trouble, for the day of battle and war? —Job 38:4, 22–23

WHEN THE LORD SPEAKS to Job, he speaks from a whirlwind. The voice in the whirlwind tells Job he is powerless before natural forces that he can neither control nor comprehend. In an age when we fiddle genetically with crops and finger the trigger of nuclear fission, God's speech may seem merely metaphorical, an allusion to vague spiritual mysteries rather than to things like plate tectonics, which—sorry, God—we have begun to fathom. It is precisely by abandoning a posture of reverential awe that we have been able to plumb the depths. Once you understand something, you can begin to control it and make it serve your purposes.

Our understanding of weather, though, has given us precious little control. It just happens. With our satellite vision we can see it coming, but we cannot keep it from happening. All we can do is run away or batten down. When the air has cleared, we know once more, like people in the wake of a hurricane or a flood, that the preacher in Ecclesiastes was right—all is vanity: "Everything before them is vanity, since one fate comes to all, to the righteous and the wicked, to the good and the evil, to the clean and the unclean, to him who sacrifices and him who does not sacrifice.... Like fish which are taken in a net and like birds which are caught in a snare, so the sons of men are snared at an evil time, when it suddenly falls upon them."

There is something deep in human nature that refuses to submit to that kind of fatalism, a refusal that goes way back before the invention of science. Fishermen of the Shetland Islands believed they could control the winds by the magical use of knots. In South Africa, a Xhosa priest-diviner would gather his people around him on a hill, fill his mouth with a special potion, and spit into the eye of the wind. In Borneo, the Kayan people drew their swords every time they heard thunder. In old Sumatra, the Batta rushed from their houses and assaulted the storm with swords and lances. In New Guinea, the Kai people threatened the wind with clubs and shouted, "If you enter my house, I'll beat your feet flat." The Cherokee stretched out their hands to push the wind in a new direction. Vanity.

In these latter days, bad weather is addressed not by warriors or priests, but by committees of scientists. In the seventies, a Weather Modification Advisory Board was called into being, a think tank that came up with an idea for taming hurricanes. Hurricanes begin as tropical storms, with the highest velocity winds farthest from the center. As warm air below stokes more and more energy into the system, the swirling air is pulled into a tight coil. The more energy the storm sucks off the ocean, the more violent it gets. It is hard to believe that an action so locally destructive could contribute to global homeostasis, but hurricanes function as automatic pressure relief valves that carry excess heat and moisture away from the tropics.

The theory was to seed the center of the storm with silver iodide to displace the ring of ascending air, a maneuver that would not kill the storm but that might loosen its coiled force. The board labeled its experiment Project Stormfury and conducted some inconclusive tests in the Atlantic. They mocked up models on the computer, and again the results were inconclusive. One definition of weather is a hell of a lot of variables. So Project Stormfury turned to the Western Pacific, where most of the earth's fifty annual hurricanes occur. The U.S. asked its Asian neighbors if they would mind a great deal if the Weather Modification Advisory Board did

a little fiddling with typhoons off their shores. The Filipinos
and the Chinese of Taiwan said they would not mind; the
Japanese and the mainland Chinese said they would. So it
looks like we will never gather enough data to know whether
or not silver iodide works as Valium for hurricanes. Probably just as well. When Americans started taking Valium in a
big way, it turned out to have unforeseen side effects.

Still, we have always been an incorrigibly optimistic people, even when it comes to bad weather. In January 1777,
George Washington was knee-deep in mud and unable to
bring his encumbered artillery to repel the advancing troops
of Charles Cornwallis. Then the wind veered to the northwest, the weather suddenly became cold, and the ground,
lately difficult for artillery, was soon frozen hard. Washington quickly deployed his forces and dealt the British two swift
defeats at Princeton and Trenton, defeats that led directly to
the surrender of Cornwallis at the siege of Yorktown a few
years later. The Americans, understandably, saw the change
in weather at that turning point in the War of Independence
as a providential act of God, a sign of His favor.

In the century that followed the revolution, thousands of
emigrants pushed across the North American wilderness. Starting at Independence, Missouri, as most of those who embarked
for California did, the settlers faced a 2,500-mile trek over an
interminable prairie, three mountain ranges, frequent and for-
midable rivers, and half a dozen deserts. Heavy rains churned
the continent into deep mud, and when the rains stopped, they
left a "tomb-like silence," in the words of one sojourner. Once
past the Continental Divide, the emigrants were a thousand

miles from Independence and more than a thousand from the Pacific. There was no turning back: they had to make it to the coast before winter. If they miscalculated by a day, as the ill-fated Donner Party did, they faced impenetrable snowfall, freezing temperatures, and slow death by starvation. Even for less adventurous souls who remained behind on homesteads in Minnesota and the Dakotas, surviving winter was a gamble. It still is.

In Minnesota, we don't have thunderous surf or steep canyons with roaring cataracts, but we do have weather. The state is smack in the middle of the North American continent, far from the moderating influences of an ocean. Summer temperatures can reach one hundred degrees, and coupled with high humidity can spawn thunderstorms and tornadoes. Everyone in the state knows someone who can tell a first-hand story about a tornado, and some of these have become part of our oral history: the twister that picked up a carton of eggs, carried it into the next county, and set it down without so much as cracking a shell. The one that lifted a locomotive train off the tracks, turned it around, and put it back down on the tracks pointing in the opposite direction.

Tornadoes work with a surgical hand, while thunderstorms swing a broad Paul Bunyan ax across the prairie, sparks jetting from the supercharged blade. An ordinary summer afternoon thunderstorm has the energy equivalent of thirteen Nagasaki-type bombs. That is not a trope; it's a scientific calculation.

Then there is winter.

Snow can fall as early as October and as late as May. There have been times in March when I have wanted to invoke the ancient custom of the Inuit in the Canadian Arctic. When the wind blew for weeks on end and they despaired of ever going out to hunt again, they made a whip of seaweed and struck out in the direction of the gale, crying, "Taba! it is enough." We humans are Pleistocene people, born sometime during the last six hundred thousand years in an ice epoch, and some of us are still there, like Shackleton, recording our dismay in a private journal.

Minnesotans know weather statistics the way baseball fans know the history of the home team. The average date of the first occurrence of thirty-two degrees Fahrenheit or lower in the fall. The average date of occurrence of the first one-inch snow accumulation. "Normal" snowfall during a "typical" winter. Average low temperatures, average high temperatures. Whenever I am told that Eskimos have one hundred words for snow, I think, "So few?" And, like sports fans, we have our rankings: high wind warning, weather advisory, winter storm watch, winter storm warning, blizzard. Snowstorms are 1. a nuisance, 2. plowable, 3. crippling.

We have refined our accommodations, of course. Highways are cleared quickly, through streets and back roads may take longer. Everyone knows to carry in the trunk:
- blankets and dried food
- a container of sand or rock salt
- battery jumper cables
- a flashlight
- matches and a candle.

We know never to change a tire with gloveless hands in subzero temperatures, lest skin fuse to metal. We listen to weather reports not just for the temperature, but for the wind-chill factor. With a wind chill of minus fifty, exposed flesh can freeze in a minute or two; at minus seventy, it's dangerous to be outside even if one is properly dressed.

We keep informed. A twenty-four-hour forecast has an accuracy of about eighty-seven percent; the fifth day of an extended forecast is fifty-six percent accurate. We are grateful for the polar-orbiting satellites that keep track of ice and cloudiness around the earth, especially the jet stream from the Northwest. Alberta Clippers can travel forty miles an hour, preceded by snow-laden winds up to sixty miles an hour. I've climbed a mountain with ropes and pitons and have gotten into one or two tight spots, but if I had to choose between heading up a thousand-foot rock face or driving through an Alberta Clipper, visibility zero, I would want to think long and hard before deciding.

If we lived on Jupiter, twice as much heat would be coming out from under our feet as would be coming in from the sun. Jupiter is ninety-nine percent hydrogen and helium, a sea of gas on a globe of liquid whirling through ten-hour days, whipping up furious storms with clouds of ammonia ice crystals. Mercury has what might be called anti-weather, airless geological death, nothing but craters, zits on a skull. We couldn't sneeze if we wanted to. And Mars: dust storms don't sweep through mere deserts or prairies, they close like a fist on the planet. There is just one season on Venus: fire and brimstone. Literally. The only rain is acid rain, sulfuric acid. No wonder it rotates backwards.

That's one way we pass the time in Minnesota. We think of places where the weather is worse.

Which is why enclosed malls were invented. When Donald Dayton, head of the Dayton department stores, commissioned a study of weather patterns in Minnesota and learned that there are only 126 "ideal shopping weather" days, he decided to do something about it.

"We plan to make our own weather at Southdale," he announced in 1952. "Every day will be fair and mild."

When Southdale opened, it was graced by a twenty-one-foot-high cage in which sixty kinds of birds sang and swooped in a perpetual spring. Three hundred and sixty-five ideal weather shopping days, year after year after year.

This ambition to manufacture ideal weather is as old as the original European arcades, the ancestors of Southdale. Charles Fourier, a writer admired by Marx and Engels, was an implacable opponent of capitalism. In 1789, when he was still an awkward provincial, he visited that granddaddy of all malls, the Palais Royal. He was dazzled.

"The first time you see it," he wrote to his mother, "you think you have entered a fairy palace." The memory of that fairy palace stayed with him his whole life. Later, when he imagined a socialist utopia, he imagined a community centered around a "Phalanstery," a colossal building adorned with "a multitude of colonnades, domes and peristyles." The Phalanstery would be connected to adjacent buildings by raised and covered passageways that would enable people "to pass through the workshops, stables, storehouses, ballrooms, banquet and assembly halls, etc., in January without knowing whether it is rainy or windy, hot or cold." The members of this utopia would stroll about in the most inclement weather "dressed in light clothes and colored shoes without worrying about the mud or the cold." Fourier produced thousands of pages of detailed blueprints of this visionary structure and attempted, unsuccessfully, to build it. It is not, however, an impossible project. It's just taking a little longer than Fourier thought it would.

There is a bronze plaque outside The Nature Company (S 128) that reads:

> The Nature Company owes its vision to the world's great naturalists: Charles Darwin, Henry David Thoreau, John Muir, David Brower, Rachael Carlson, Jacques Cousteau, and many others. Through this inspiration, we are dedicated to providing products and experiences which encourage the joyous observation, understanding, and appreciation of the world of nature.... Our goal is to provide you with products, insights, and experiences which kindle your own sense of wonder and which will help you feel good about yourself and the world in which you live. We hope you enjoy your visit.

To the right of the plaque, positioned in the store's entrance, is a three-foot inflated penguin. New Age music—panpipes mingled with wind and rain—resonate throughout the interior.

The first thing I come upon is a display of "animal sounds" key chains. Each key chain has a plastic image of a frog, a bird, or a cricket, and if you press the image, it emits the sound of a frog, a bird, or a cricket. There are tins of wild animal cookies. Butterfly seed mix "contains nine colorful nectar-producing flower varieties to attract butterflies through the summer." There are men's ties with acorn patterns. Eagles and kestrels are not stuffed and mounted but cast in porcelain, small enough to hold in the hand. There are lovely rocks and petrified wood, T-shirts, and posters, gorgeous posters. Running Deer Ranch apricot preserves and Rainforest candy. Also rain-forest frog shower curtains, with bright images of the black and green frog, the Kokoa-Pa frog, the dyeing frog, the blue poison arrow frog, the Granula frog, the Lehman's frog. There are frog puppets and frog marionettes. There are yo-yos.

Lots of tapes to put you back in the wild even as you are locked in rush-hour traffic. Wolf Talk. Glacier Bay. Mountain Stream. Cloud Forest. A three-tape set: Gentle Ocean, Morning Songbirds, Distant Thunder. There are shelves and shelves of books on every imaginable natural subject, more data than the mind can hold. Technical books about meteorology and mystical books about Giving Voice to Bear. On my way out, I notice a pile of huggable cloth whales.

There seems to be no limit to the marketing of wildlife and wilderness. Remember the fire that destroyed 793,880 acres in Yellowstone back in 1988? Everyone was furious, the local merchants robbed of their income, the tourists deprived of a recreational opportunity, all because guys in

Smokey Bear hats thought a controlled fire would be good for the forest—it would clear out the deadwood. This one got a little out of control because of crazy weather. Naturally folks got angry. The whole point of a Park Service is to manage things like that.

Well, it turns out the Smokey Bears were right after all. What appeared to be a disaster has turned out to be not only a boon to the land but a boost to tourism, because the dramatic traces of fire added to its natural beauty. Over the years the black-on-black color scheme of the post-fire park has softened, as the charred bark peels from the trees and the Madison, Gibbon, and Yellowstone rivers have carried the ash away. For generations of baby boomers educated to appreciate the color fields of Mark Rothko, the park is once again picture perfect. Motels and gift shops are selling "Yellowstone Aflame" videos. The Park Service can once again say to vacationing taxpayers, as the Nature Company says to its customers, "Our goal is to provide you with products, insights, and experiences which will kindle your sense of wonder and which will help you feel good about yourself and the world in which you live."

At the Endangered Species store (N 255), you can buy a fuzzy toy or poster or T-shirt of a creature on the edge of extinction. I guess the concept is that even if the animal perishes, its image will live on.

Colorado (N 282) also has a mission statement displayed at its entrance: "The idea is functional yet fashionable. Apparel and footwear that reflect the 'Great Outdoors.' And the personalities of those who wear them. Remember, Colorado isn't only a store; it's a state...a state of mind." Inside, bleached linen overhead suggests a tent, but you can't actually buy a tent in Colorado. You have to go to one of the three Eddie Bauer stores (W 230-234): Eddie Bauer, Casual Wear and Outfitting; Eddie Bauer, the Look; Eddie Bauer, Home Collectibles, furnishings for your condo in the wild. There are no tents in stock at Eddie Bauer, Casual Wear and Outfitting, but they will order one for you from their catalog.

The wilderness trekker theme appears throughout the Mall, though in some of the upscale stores, such as Abercrombie and Fitch (N 200), it has been refined into Old Money flannel or denim. Malls have deconstructed the old indoor-outdoor opposition. The "Great Outdoors" is a look, an attitude. Colorado is a state of mind.

At Butterflies and More (N 270), I can buy arrangements of butterflies to hang on a wall. I am handed a flyer which reads:

> None of the butterflies used in the panels are endangered. The butterflies used in our panels are bred on plantations, farms, and gathered from the floor of the rain forest all over the world....
>
> [We] aim to satisfy both the eyes and ears...and create a multi-sensual nourishment...in an almost mystical state of rest. Bringing people to this state is one of the goals of Butterflies and our success is the visitor's good fortune. From this state of sensual satisfaction you can quietly contemplate the butterfly compositions and choose

210

which butterfly will make its final destination in your home or office....

We support the world committees on Environmental Clean Up and Preservation of the Rain Forests.

Butterflies have always mystified me. The monarchs from my neck of the woods leave each year in late summer or early autumn and migrate 1250 to 1850 miles to wintering sites along the coast of the Gulf of Mexico or inland in Texas and Mexico. How do these exquisite insects orientate themselves? For instance, when the butterfly lights upon a field to eat and refuel, how does it invariably find its compass course when it takes off again? I got a book on animal migration once and discovered that they steer by the sun's azimuth (the point on the horizon directly below the sun's disc), maintaining a preferred angle to its movement across the horizon, adjusting their flight as well to temperature and the strength and direction of prevailing winds. Yet how can they possibly have the navigational technology in their tiny little bodies to bring this journey off? Learning from experience is out of the question, for they live no more than four or five months. Is it a matter of group-think, such as one can find in other insect species? If so, it's still very mysterious; and yet, despite the monarchs' skills as voyagers, skills that far surpass our own genetic capacity for transcontinental flight, it is extremely unlikely that they have a subjective life. It's hard to imagine that their trip is much of an "experience" for them, though I suppose we will never know for certain.

Here at Butterflies and More, their diaphanous bodies, "gathered from the floor of rain forests all over the world," are arranged into lovely patterns of flight, like New Age music for the eye, balm for the soul we're not sure we have. If I bought one of these Plexiglas boxes and hung it in my living room, could I count on it to put me into a "state of sensual satisfaction," as the handout promises? If I were sipping my third glass of Chardonnay, it might. If I kept sipping and gazing I might even find myself "in an almost mystical state of rest." But right now, stone sober, I'm thinking of some lines from T. S. Eliot's "The Love Song of J. Alfred Prufrock."

> And when I am formulated, sprawling on a pin,
> When I am pinned and wriggling on the wall,
> Then how should I begin
> To spit out all the butt-ends of my days and ways?

I suspect there may be dimensions to the ecosystem we haven't begun to fathom.

———

At Recycle Now (W 304), I learn that Browning-Ferris Industries Recycling Services intends to recycle more than seventy-five tons of waste material per week at the Mall of America, which is more than fifty percent of the waste generated. (That estimate fell far short of the actual waste produced.) Display panels pose riddles. Q. How many grocery bags are made from one twenty-year-old tree? A. 700. Q. What is the #1 recreational pursuit in America? A. Gardening. Q. The junk mail that Americans receive in one day could produce enough energy to heat how many homes? A. 250,000.

Every year on the third week of October, the Mall and Browning-Ferris sponsor several days of "Ecommunity, a festival of environmental education and fun" with "Ecogames" for children. Special exhibits have featured sculpture made from recycled paper products, a maze constructed from recycled plastic, "found art" and art made from "cast-off materials" by local artists. In 1993 a mammoth four-story globe, created by schoolchildren from all over Minnesota, was displayed in the rotunda. There was a town meeting on "Building Sustainable Communities," at which "internationally recognized dignitaries" were present.

On a less solemn occasion, the subject of sustainable communities was taken up by a fairy princess. She had ensconced herself rather regally in Bloomingdale's court and was reading a story, "Lots and Lots of Pippindotz," to a dozen children seated around her. She told them of a world full of magical dotz that could be soft or hard, light or heavy, clear or colorful. In the story, a wise old figure, "the Chancellah from a far off land," explained the many uses of these dotz.

> Well, the things those dotz do
> total more than a few.
> Your lunchbox for starters—it's sensibly strong
> Because of those dotz, it lasts very long.
> And that tuna you smacked, no freshness it lacked,
> because of those dotz, the wrap stayed intact....
> and over there not very far,
> inside and outside that little red car
> Those dotz get blended into bumpers unbended.

The trick, according to this wise creature, is to keep recycling everything. That way we can consume all the merchandise we want and save the rain forests. And live happily ever after. In Pippindotz. The sustainable community.

———

The World's Most Ancient Intact Animal
Discovered in Russia!
Now in Minnesota!
Mall of America!!

So read the flyer touting "The World of Mammoths," a natural history exhibit of the Ice Age, from the St. Petersburg Museum in Russia and part of the Mall of America's gala opening. Housed on the first floor at East Broadway and North Garden, it ran from August 11 to December 31, though I didn't get to it until December. The exhibit's hundred specimens were refugees from the recently concluded Cold War, Eurasian visitors who were able to thaw out for a few months in a free-market sanctuary. The star of this traveling troupe was DIMA, a baby mammoth discovered by a gold prospector in June, 1977, at a depth of seven feet in a layer of frozen ground in Siberia. DIMA, still in her skin, looked like a partially inflated leather replica, a rich kid's oversized huggable toy from F.A.O. Schwartz (W 134). Depending on how you reckoned her age, she was seven or eight months old or forty thousand years old. There was also the assembled skeleton of a fully grown woolly mammoth, about sixteen feet tall, with great sweeping tusks. Nothing but bones and air now, it had once weighed about seven tons.

Bits and pieces of other exotic creatures hung on walls or were encased in glass: the skull of a woolly rhinoceros (once widespread in Europe and Northern Asia); the skull and mummified legs of a wild horse of the Ice Age; the skull of a Pleistocene bison; the skull of an ancestral cow; the skull of a giant Pleistocene deer, misnamed the Irish elk in the West. There were also whole-bodied, fully clothed examples of Arctic rabbits, foxes, wolves, owls, all sorts of winged and footed critters, stuffed survivors, I guess you'd call them, of species that are not yet extinct.

Visitors tended to cluster around the life forms that had long since disappeared, perhaps because they had disappeared, perhaps because they were, even in these attenuated shapes, magnificent. The longer you gazed at them the more mysterious they became. They were certainly mysterious to our ancestors, who painted their forms on walls deep inside caves. How did these cousins of the elephant and the rhinoceros ever wander onto the tundra? Why in the world did they decide to stay in such a climate? How did they persist through the long winters, thousands of them? And why did they grow so big? Heat is lost from the surface of the body, so the smaller the body's surface relative to its volume the better its energy conservation. Because long, thin extremities are easily chilled, it helps to have small ears and short limbs. These factors are particularly crucial in warm-blooded animals; their highly complex organs cannot tolerate more than a few degrees' variation in temperature. To make it through a long, cold winter, one ought, ideally, to be a large sphere or cube—hence the woolly mammoth, the Russian peasant, the igloo, and the Mall of America. The polar bear and grizzly are the largest bears, the moose the largest deer, the wolverine the largest weasel. But there's a limit.

Size has its costs. Take the mammoth's only surviving cousin, the elephant. It requires an acre of lung surfaces to absorb oxygen, an eight-foot trunk to reach its food, a massive heart to circulate its blood, and hundreds of feet of guts and complex digestive organs to extract nourishment from the hundreds of pounds of foliage and grass it eats during its daily sixteen hours of browsing. A huge mammal requires constant and abundant supplies of fuel. No problem for an African elephant, who lives, botanically speaking, in hog heaven. A bit of a problem, though, for a woolly mammoth grazing in a Siberian winter.

When you're as big as an elephant, you have to keep moving just to eat; and when you're a woolly mammoth, you need to keep moving to stay warm as well. That presents another challenge. Whereas high volume to low surface is helpful in retaining energy, it makes movement difficult. Try to imagine a three-hundred-pound athlete winning any track event, whatever the distance. The force of gravity would be too great a handicap. On the moon, however, you might have to weigh at least three hundred pounds to even attempt a serious 440 dash. On the moon, a woolly mammoth could scamper about on spidery legs and a woolly rhinoceros could leap like a grasshopper. It's too late, though, to consider such an experiment. Of the 352 known species of proboscideans (mastodons, mammoths, etc.) that have roamed the earth in the last few million years, only two survive—the African and Indian elephants.

Seen in this context, the Mall of America represents an impressive adaptation to frigid conditions. It is massive and squat, low to the ground (relatively speaking), and without slender extremities. It doesn't have to forage for energy; it doesn't have to move at all. Indeed, movement of any kind would be fatal. It's as if Moby Dick, beached in the Great Plains, discovered that life on the prairie is far less cutthroat than in the Atlantic: simply open your maw and consume the rich lichen blown your way by the foul climate. This new leviathan, of course, needs a caretaker with a state-of-the-art pooper-scooper.

Size, without question, has its advantages. Consider those gorgeous tusks on the woolly mammoth, sixteen-foot horns that sweep outward, then curve back toward the its skull. How, you might ask, could they possibly have enhanced the animal's prospects for survival? They are far too cumbersome to be used as weapons. The same question is prompted by the humungus antlers of the Irish elk, which roamed Siberia with the woolly mammoth during the Pleistocene. This elk wasn't really Irish. It wasn't even an elk; it was a giant deer, the biggest ever. And the biggest thing about it was its broad-palmed antlers, with a twelve-foot span. The giant deer skull on display in the Mall of America exhibit didn't have antlers attached, but I've seen pictures of them: awesome. These horns were allometric; they increased two and a half times as much as the skull's length. Why did natural selection favor monster deer with Mount Rushmore headgear?

Scientists have long pondered this conundrum and have come up with any number of answers. The most likely explanation is that the antlers, like the mammoth tusks, were not actual but only symbolic weapons, structures used for ritual-ized behavior that established rank and hierarchy. If it is apparent to all that you are the biggest (and therefore the best), you are seldom challenged to defend your turf. The male lion sleeps throughout the day and bestirs himself only to eat and copulate. Elvis no longer bothers to perform on stage. In these instances, kingship is demonstrated by a thick head of hair, a later mutation of the broad-palmed antlers. The Mall of America flourishes as yet another variant, stars and stripes ascendant, the ultimate emblem of dominance and power.

"Big buildings are complicated beasts," a friend remarked to me recently. He's the director of a research center at the University of Minnesota devoted to a new field called "building science," and he meant that the operations that sustain a building are elaborate and extensive, a maze of micro-computer systems managing hundreds of processes. Three-fourths of the energy required by a heating-ventilating system in a modern air-conditioned building, for instance, is used just to circulate the air. In the dead of winter, a skyscraper or a mall needs to dissipate the excess heat pouring from its inner core—lights, computers, motors, people—so it draws in cold air from the outside.

Buildings have their alimentary canals, of course, through which they move their liquid and solid wastes. In the case of the Mall of America, that amounts to six hundred tons a month, the amount of waste that would be produced by a population of 65,000 wooly mammoths. (Your modern average Homo sapiens americanus generates slightly more garbage than three times the daily waste of a Pleistocene pachyderm.)

These devices evolved under the pressures of natural selection. The skeleton, for example, mutated from an outer shell to an inner supporting frame both in buildings (steel) and animals (bones), and in both this change made possible a considerable increase in anatomical size. At my friend's research center, there are design teams made up of engineers and architects who think of buildings primarily in terms of energy and can punch a blueprint into a computer and simulate its probable metabolism. They are working on what is called "green technology," technology that produces minimal damage and depletion in the environment. Green technology, economists and scientists tell us, is more than a marketing concept; our nation's economic survival may depend on our capacity to create such innovations.

The survivors of the Pleistocene tended to be modest in size—the beaver, the caribou, the hyena, the deer, the fox, the wolf—yet our free market appears to favor monster life forms. Still...I look at the shimmering skyscrapers in Minneapolis and at the malls encircling them and I wonder: will these gorgeous creatures go the way of the woolly mammoth and the Irish elk, pummeled by unforgiving weather into fragments at an archeological exhibit for alien children a thousand years from now? It's too soon to tell, but stranger things have happened.

———

Next to Bloomingdale's, the Rainforest Cafe seems to sweep you inside whether you want to be swept in or not. The colorful logo overhead, chock-full of animal faces, promises "A Wild Place to Eat and Shop," and the sweatshirts proclaim "An Environmentally Conscious Family Adventure," but those slogans don't begin to describe the atmosphere here. Trader Vic's meets Disney World would be more like it. A life-size Disney 'gator, head swinging back and forth, jaws opening and clamping shut. If children throw coins into the water on which the 'gator floats, as they are invited to do, "All donations will go to charities that help to rescue the rainforest." There are a few live critters here and there— exotic fish in aquariums, exotic birds in a cage—but ninety-eight percent of the flora and fauna in this ecosystem is fake. The retail space is dominated by a huge tree trunk composed of plastic, oversized oranges, lemons, limes, pineapples, bananas, pears, grapes, cherries, and an avocado. The parrots and macaws, though, are the genuine article.

The juice bar offers fresh fruit and root juices, organic breads, coffees, pastries. Among the "Designer Juices" available: Amazon Energy (a blend of carrot and apple), Blue Mountain Sunrise (carrot, beet, and apple—"jump start your heart") and the Medicine Man (carrot, celery, and apple— "good for the liver and pancreas"). The wary novice is assured, "Don't Panic It's Organic." The cafe itself is equally innovative. My favorite on the adult menu: Gorillas in the Mist ("A Monte Cristo style peanut butter and jelly sandwich, sprinkled with powdered sugar"). My favorite on the children's menu: Jurassic Chicken Tidbits ("Natural chicken pieces in the shape of dinosaurs").

Patrons enjoy this fare surrounded by fake trees with dense foliage overhead, a starlit night breaking through, toy monkeys hanging down, some animated, some not. Fake rocks, water falling over them. A dayglo rainbow. A bronze larger-than-life native (a composite of racial types) bows beneath a globe lit up with green and blue neon lights. Every twenty minutes, thunder rumbles through the restaurant. A saxophone wails jazz in the background. Did the natives who put all this together live on a diet of magic mushrooms?

Not really. Steve Schussler, the entrepreneur behind it, is a native of New York City who learned the strategies of survival in an urban ecosystem. He was eight when his parents divorced and his affluent father abandoned the family. Gone was the sixteen-room mansion, his own bedroom, his big brass bed. There were only two bedrooms in the small apartment he shared with his mother and two brothers. He grew up delivering papers, pumping gas, hustling pizzas. He had to hitchhike to football practice. He graduated halfway through his senior year; after the football season ended there didn't seem to be any point in staying around.

He headed down to Florida and moved in with his Uncle Ted, a banker in Dade County. Ted was his role model. He had been a football star and straight-A student in high school and had gone on to Harvard on scholarships. He taught Steve the habit of a disciplined life and the basics of money management. For a while Steve took classes at Miami Dade Community College at night and worked during the day as a lineman for Southern Bell. Then he said, "Screw this," packaged himself in a crate, and had the crate sent to WGBS in Miami. When they opened the crate at the radio station, Steve sprang out dressed in a Superman suit and declared, "I'm your supersalesman!" They laughed and put him to work. He sold air time and wrote copy for clients.

That was the start of a decade of leapfrogging. Steve had his own signature chutzpah. When he applied for a job at Peters, Griffen, and Woodware in Manhattan, he sent the chairman a child's plastic boat: "Welcome me aboard!" The chairman returned the boat: "Your boat has a leak." Steve sent it back: "The leak is fixed. Welcome me aboard." He got the job.

On to Chicago. A new job every eighteen months. Still selling air time. But a man that restless gets impatient working for others, and it wasn't long before Steve opened his own retail store selling the big toys he had always loved—carousel horses, juke boxes, slot machines, antique radios. He called his shop Juke Box Saturday Night. He saw it as a hobby rather than a source of income, but the autonomy and creative freedom of entrepreneurship was so seductive he spent less and less time on his bread-and-butter job. They fired him.

Then one night Jim Rittenberg, an established Chicago night club owner and promoter, came into Steve's store looking for props for a new night club with a fifties and early sixties theme. By the time he left, he had a name for his club—Juke Box Saturday Night—and a partner, Steve Schussler. Schussler and Rittenberg opened four clubs in Chicago and expanded into Des Moines, San Francisco, Minneapolis. When he was thirty, Steve was on the cover of *Entrepreneur* magazine. The story described him as "a walking, talking, breathing promo gimmick who knows instinctively what has to be done and how to make it happen."

Five years later, he was bankrupt. Juke Box Saturday Night, overextended, collapsed on itself. Steve's empire was reduced to a single club in Minneapolis, and even that was closing down. He sold everything he had, even his beloved Wurlitzer juke box, to pay off his creditors. That left him with $136 and his next dream.

It was something he had been mulling over for years. A retail-restaurant place with a rain-forest theme. The idea started with his pet parrot. In the eighties, on a vacation in Brazil, he had seen a real rain forest and thought, "Wow, this is where my parrot came from. I wonder if he misses it?" When he returned home, he started fixing up a special room for his parrot—plants, a little fountain, a plastic snake. Like Juke Box Saturday Night, the room started out as a hobby and evolved into a concept. Steve didn't have a wife or children. What he had was a parrot and a child's imagination.

When he went to potential backers with his idea for a Rainforest Cafe, they told him (according to Steve), "Fuck you. Fuck you twice." No one wanted to risk money on a proven bankrupt. This had been a lifelong challenge for Steve, getting people to see his potential. When you're dealing with men who have little or no imagination, you have to get very literal. You have to dress up in a Superman suit, you have to mail them a boat. Okay. Steve knew what he had to do.

He turned his entire house in St. Louis Park into the Rainforest Cafe. The entire house: bedrooms, living room, dining room, kitchen. Not even the bathroom was a refuge from the plastic rocks, plants, stuffed animals, and forty *live* parrots. Two giant tortoises were in residence in his kitchen, where they devoured sixteen heads of lettuce a day. This hyperreality required Steve to install four generators in his backyard. He had 3,250 feet of extension cord running through his house and the highest residential electric bill in the state of Minnesota. It was a bill he was not always able to pay, and there would come a point in almost every month when Northern States Power would cut off his electricity and gas. To sustain his folly Steve had to keep borrowing money, running up a tab of half a million dollars.

Only a bachelor with no wife or children could do something like this. Needless to say, his neighbors noticed. They trained their binoculars on his windows and exchanged speculation and gossip about each new extravagance. They called him "the crazy professor," though Steve Schussler is about as far from being a professor as one can be. He took their interest in his affairs good-naturedly and they knew that whenever they knocked on his door, for whatever fabricated reason, they would get yet another impromptu tour.

They were not the only ones taking an interest. Federal agents raided his home on the assumption that any residence using that much light must be a covert marijuana farm. They left weeping with laughter.

Every weekend Steve invited potential investors to his house to see his dream. What's so special about this, they asked, apart from the over-the-top craziness? Combining eating and retail was hardly new. And what about those live parrots? Who wants bird shit in his Caesar salad? It's not the live parrots, Steve tried to explain, it's the live parrots *and* the silicon monkeys. It's actual tropical fish and virtual talking trees.

Steve would not have put it this way, but he was trying to get his prospective backers to image a postmodern rain forest—not a virgin rain forest, but something sexier, even, in a totally family way, of course, just a little bit kinky. He was spinning the Camp Snoopy idea—fake rocks and real trees, a stuffed dog and live raptors in one boisterous menagerie—but not just as a kid thing.

A tape of whale songs can induce alpha waves in rush-hour gridlock; butterflies on the wall of your home or office may, just may, lift you from fast-track stress to "an almost mystical state of rest." Colorado, after all, is a state of mind. And nature itself is a warehouse with a vast inventory of marketable images, sounds, even smells. (Steve would pump fresh flower extract into Rainforest's retail store.) As our ecological crisis deepens, the nostalgic appeal and commercial values of these commodities can only increase. It's the old idea of the garden (nature brought closer to human desire), repackaged for a new millennium. "A Wild Place to Eat and Shop." With a little faith, Steve told his guests, the Rainforest Cafe might reforest the urban world.

They chuckled at his enthusiasm, his parrots and gimcrackery, they slapped him on the back, and they told him to call them which his concept was open for business. They were not about to throw away serious money on this project, but it would be a hoot to visit it...once. Steve waved them good-bye and went back to his kitchen and his tortoises and rethought all he had done. Was there a new possibility he hadn't yet imagined? This was fun.

Since the day it opened in 1994, the Rainforest Cafe has been one of the big successes of the Mall of America. There is usually a line outside the restaurant, and on busy days you may have to wait three hours for a table. Fortunately you're in the perfect place to kill time. Steve and his partners (he did find some eventually) went public after one year. No shortage of investors now. Rainforest Cafes began sprouting like fantastical kudzu all over the U.S. and throughout the world—in Mexico, Asia, Europe.

Successful marketing concepts, like successful species in the wild, reproduce rapidly. The in-your-face artifice of the Rainforest Cafe, no less than the Kokoa-Pa frog, is a product of natural selection. A rain forest, unlike an Arctic tundra, is an environment richly supportive of life, a thick soup of exotic flora and fauna. In a square mile, you won't find a dozen different species of tree, but hundreds. The challenge here is excessive abundance rather than inhospitable climate or scarcity of nutrients. Every square inch is fought over. The tiniest adaptive edge is the difference between survival and death, and mutation is forever rolling the dice. Today's advantage may not be an advantage tomorrow.

Steve's earlier club, Juke Box Saturday Night, went belly up in Minneapolis because of unpredictable changes in its environment, some of them big (a convention center closed for two and one-half years for renovation, a three-percent tax on entertainment, the competition of newer clubs and restaurants), some of them small (an increase in parking fees). The Rainforest Cafe is more than holding its own against the competition, but that could change in a twinkling. The Mall of

America, with more than five hundred stores and eateries, is a teeming free market ecosystem where the margin of error is very slight. Its roster of clients is always changing. For the time being, Steve Schussler, who studied Darwin in the school of hard knocks, has found a niche in its neon jungle.

———

Outside, the wind chill could snap a bone in two, but in the Mall of America this Saturday morning it's officially "Fun in the Sun." Summertime boats drift at anchor all over the Mall, seven in the West Market entrance alone. Sleek, aerodynamic vessels with names like "Islander," "Ebbtide," and "Outlaw" and 150 and 200 Pro V Yamaha engines. The Outlaw must be forty feet long, white with bold streaks of yellow, aqua, rose, and magenta. There is a cherry red pontoon in front of Sears, and at the entrance to Nordstrom a Baja 180 Islander: custom bucket seats, ice chest, white vinyl rub rails, swing-down ladder, sun deck, cockpit lighting, Mere cruiser 4.3 L x engine, "water ready." Yours for only $13,995. At Bloomingdale's there are ten "Bombardiers," brightly painted craft that look like snowmobiles for summer lakes.

Kids are strolling around in T-shirts; the Good Humor ice cream truck is doing a brisk business. The trees are mainly tropical—orange jasmine, black olive, oleanders, hibiscus—and in the perpetual summer of Camp Snoopy (forever seventy degrees), the paths are edged with rhododendrons, willow figs, Buddhist pines, and azaleas native to Florida, Georgia, and Mississippi. The roller coaster, the Screaming Yellow Eagle, the Balloon Race are in full swing. Brilliant sunlight pours down from the glass roof overhead. At Macy's Court they have assembled a seventeen-foot "Mountain in the Mall," a four-sided peak made out of powdered granite and epoxy glue with lots of footholds. Children are lined up to get strapped into nylon ropes and attempt some novice rock climbing.

I make my way to the rotunda for the morning's main event, a Pro Impact Women's Volleyball Exhibition. A twenty-five-foot net is stretched across a sea-blue court. The women are already warming up when I arrive, sleek and agile as predatory cats in their T-shirts and Lycra shorts and knee guards, all but one deeply tanned. When the teams are introduced—the Crystal Pepsis vs. the Vibrant Shampoos—they all turn out to be California girls except for the pale blonde who is from Minneapolis. I watch the back and forth for a while, the score lit up in neon numbers on the board, then drift off again. I notice on the schedule of events that there was a beachwear fashion show last Saturday in the rotunda. A missed opportunity.

It's hard to believe there's a brutal winter just beyond the wall: out of sight, out of mind. I pay brief homage to Donald Dayton and Arthur Gruen and their vision of 365 ideal shopping days. What had Gruen said at the opening of South-dale? "It can be one hundred degrees above or twenty degrees below zero—things which I understand happen in Minnesota. But here flowers will grow, birds will sing, and it's going to be spring."

There are losses as well as gains, however, when we retreat into a world of our own making. When Nature turns terrible, she shakes us from our complacency. The presence of terror, the Romantics felt, distinguishes the sublime from the merely beautiful. They sought the sublime in the mountains and by the ocean, but it is found not only there. In *The Long Winter,* Laura Ingalls Wilder tells of a terrible season on the Great Plains when blizzard followed blizzard from October to April. One evening, though, Laura listens to the howling wind with different ears. It is after supper. Her father calls for his fiddle and Laura brings it to him.

> But when he had tuned the strings and rosined the bow he played a strange melody. The fiddle moaned a deep, rushing undertone and wild notes flickered high above it, rising until they thinned away in nothingness, only to come wailing back, the same notes but not quite the same, as if they had been changed while out of hearing.
>
> Queer shivers tingled up Laura's backbone and prickled over her scalp, and still the wild, changing melody came from the fiddle till she couldn't bear it and cried, "What is it, Pa? Oh, what is that tune?"
>
> "Listen." Pa stopped playing and held his bow still, above the string. "The tune is outdoors. I was only following it."

Laura encounters that terrible beauty in the prairie's silence as well.

> Everything was still. No wind stirred the grey-bleached grass and no birds were on the water or in the sky. The lake faintly lapped at the rim of that stillness.
>
> Laura looked at Pa and she knew he was listening too. The silence was as terrible as cold is. It was stronger than any sound. It could stop the water's lapping and the

thin, faint ringing in Laura's ears. The silence was no sound, no movement, no thing; that was its terror. Laura's heart jumped and jumped, trying to get away from it.

In Pa's music and in the stillness, Laura hears the voice that spoke to Job. It is not a voice one hears in the Mall of America.

Chapter Ten

The Underground
Man

IN 1851 A STRUCTURE OF CAST IRON and glass was erected in
London's Hyde Park to house the one hundred thousand
exhibits of the Great Exhibition of the Works of Industry of
All Nations. Its proportions were staggering: almost three quar-
ters of a million square feet at ground level, nearly a quarter
of a million in the galleries. The barrel-vaulted transept was
408 feet long and 104 feet high at the center. Dismantled at
the close of the Exhibition, it was, according to a historian of
engineering, "the first large and truly significant building to
be made of metal and glass, the first major building to use outer
walls that provided no structural strength; and the first building constructed using prefabricated standardized units that
were shipped to the construction site for rapid assembly."

The structure was assembled in an astonishingly brief
four months. In one week, eighty glaziers put in eighteen
thousand panes of glass. At a time when railway bridges were

collapsing at such an alarming rate that a royal commission was appointed to investigate the suitability of iron as an engineering material, here was a huge iron mastodon taking shape in a twinkling. Would its vast galleries and walkways hold against the onslaught of wind and hail? The *Times* prophesied tragedy on the opening day when Queen Victoria arrived: the official salute would "shiver the roof of the Palace, and thousands of ladies will be cut to mincemeat."

In fact, the opening, on the first of May, was a stunning success. "The sight as we came to the middle was magical," Queen Victoria recorded in her journal, "so vast, so glorious, so touching." The structure absorbed as many as one hundred thousand visitors a day (six million in five months) without incident. The glass held against wind and hail. Canvas, suspended over the roof and adjusted by louvers in the walls, kept the crowds cool despite exterior heat and humidity. An expert eye would have found ingenious details everywhere: the floorboards, for example, were spaced one-half inch apart so that dirt and debris could be swept between them. (Underneath, small boys collected flammable materials.) It was christened the Crystal Palace. In our world of sumptuous suburban malls, each chock-full of the riches of commerce, the atmosphere perfectly controlled, it may be hard to appreciate how dazzling the Crystal Palace was in its day. It honored the achievement of rational, economic planning and it promised even greater triumphs, not just in industrial engineering but in social engineering as well.

The Palace was such a triumph that at the conclusion of the Great Exhibition (the first World's Fair), it was moved to a new site on London's southern outskirts, where it was considerably enlarged. Here is one writer's description of the result:

> When built, it was filled with extraordinary objects: courts representing the different periods in the history of art, hundreds of sculptures—some of them colossal—trees, art galleries, a hall of fame, a theater, a concert hall with four thousand seats and room in the centre for a Grand Orchestra of four thousand musicians and a Great Organ with 4,500 pipes.
>
> The Crystal Palace at Sydenham was not a museum, or a concert hall, or a huge park; it was all three at once, perhaps the first example of what are today called theme parks. A family could spend the whole day there, enjoying the setting and spectacle and finishing in the evening with a huge fireworks display for which the place became famous. It was here, too, that a large audience first watched moving pictures. There were balloon ascents, high-wire acts, shows, exhibitions, conferences, pantomimes, and spectacular events such as the staging of an invasion in which an entire village was destroyed in front of twenty-five thousand spectators. The Crystal Palace provided for the first time a leisure center where people from any background could enjoy their free time.

The Crystal Palace flourished well into this century, and then, in 1936, in the depth of the Great Depression, this legendary monument to industrial capitalism burned to the ground. Its demise seemed to symbolize a larger crisis of faith.

There had been skeptics of the Crystal Palace and all it stood for from the very beginning, however. One was a mousy little bureaucrat who, by his own admission, was a neurotic. "I am a sick man. I am a spiteful man. I am an unpleasant man." In his *Notes from Underground*, Dostoevsky called him the Underground Man. "As far as my own personal opinion is concerned," he declared, "to care only for prosperity seems to me somehow ill-bred. Whether it's good or bad, it is sometimes very pleasant to smash things, too. After all, I do not really insist on suffering or on prosperity either. I insist on my caprice, and its being guaranteed to me when necessary. Suffering would be out of place in vaudevilles, for instance; I know that. In the Crystal Palace it is even unthinkable; suffering means doubt, means negation, and what would be the good of a Crystal Palace if there could be any doubt about it? And yet I am sure man will never renounce real suffering, that is, destruction and chaos. Why, after all, suffering is the sole origin of consciousness.... You believe in a crystal edifice that can never be destroyed; that is, an edifice at which one would neither be able to stick out one's tongue nor thumb one's nose on the sly. And perhaps I am afraid of this edifice just because it is of crystal and can never be destroyed and that one could not even put one's tongue out at it even on the sly."

The Underground Man went on and on in this vein: "Now I ask you: What can you expect from man since he is a creature endowed with such strange qualities? Shower upon him every earthly blessing, drown him in bliss so that nothing but bubbles would dance on the surface of his bliss, as on a sea; give him such economic prosperity that he would have nothing else to do but sleep, eat cakes and busy himself with ensuring the continuation of world history and even then man, out of sheer ingratitude, sheer libel, would play you some loathsome trick. He would even risk his cakes and would deliberately desire the most fatal rubbish, the most uneconomical absurdity, simply to introduce into all this rationality his fatal fantastic elements."

His complaint in a nutshell: "Although our life, in this manifestation of it, is often worthless, yet it is life nevertheless and not simply an extraction of square roots."

An Underground Man, however, is by definition out of sight and out of mind. The industrial nations continued to march forward and to celebrate their progress in ever more extravagant world's fairs: the Paris Exposition Universelle of 1889 and the World's Columbian Exposition in Chicago in 1893 honoring the four hundredth anniversary of the discovery of the New World. Chicago turned the swamp land of Jackson Park into what became known as the White City, a shimmering utopian future done in Roman and Renaissance style, decked out with arches and columns and classically inspired sculpture. It was gorgeous to look at, and still is in archival photographs. All fake, of course: most of the structures and imposing edifices were made of plaster of Paris reinforced with steel and wood and painted to look like marble. After the fair closed, the whole thing went up in smoke, as the Crystal Palace would do half a century later. It was a fitting end. The World Columbian Exposition of 1893 had been more dream than reality.

The country, no less than the Exposition, was dry tinder waiting for a spark. The Civil War was still a fresh memory. So too were the Battle of the Little Big Horn and the massacre at Wounded Knee. At the Congress of History held at the Exposition, Frederick Turner announced that the closing of the frontier amounted to a crisis of American identity. New immigrants from middle and eastern Europe flooding into the U.S. and into Chicago itself, where they were ill-fed and ill-housed, posed enormous challenges to the nation's largest cities. Tensions between labor and management had become violent in the Haymarket Square Massacre in Chicago in 1886 and the Homestead Steel Strike of 1892. The year of the Exposition was a year of severe economic turmoil, a panic in which 491 banks and 15,000 commercial institutions failed and the country plunged into a depression that lasted until 1897. In 1893 the U.S. was hardly in a position to justify the motto on its currency, "E Pluribus Unum," much less assume global leadership.

None of this, of course, dampened the nation's celebration of Columbus's triumphant miscalculation four hundred years earlier. And once more an impossible expectation was realized: the American dream was about to define "the American century." Along the Midway, ethnographic simulations of villages from Asia, the Mideast, Africa, and the Americas led visitors through the journey of evolution to the city of the future. The Columbian Exposition, its publicity proclaimed, would be "a vast university, where the nations will become voluntary pupils and the work of their handicraft serve as object lessons for the study and benefit of all.... The children of the East can meet with those of the North, South and West, and all can learn of the advancement and progress which his fellow man has made on his respectful portion of the globe." What the U.S. had made of its portion of the globe was abundantly evident in the largest structure, the Manufactures Building. Henry Van Brunt, one of the fair's architects, observed, "In this vast orchestra, no individuality forces itself into undue prominence to disturb the majestic symphony." Playing an American score, of course.

Walt Disney, who was born in Chicago at the turn of the century, picked up this optimism and carried it into our own day. He turned the Crystal Palace and the World's Fairs that followed into the ultimate theme park, a dazzling entertainment that is also a vision of history, a vision succinctly summed up at the Carousel of Progress in Disney World.

> On this and every turn we'll be making progress. And progress is not just moving ahead. Progress is dreaming, working, building a better way of life. Progress is commitment to people. A commitment to making today and tomorrow the best time of your life. It wasn't always easy. At every turn in our history there was always someone saying, "Turn back! Turn back!" But there was no turning back. Not for us; not for our carousel. A challenge always lies ahead. And as long as man dreams and works and builds together, these years, too, can be the best time of your life.

The Crystal Palace was a symbol of the modern faith in perpetual material progress and human perfectibility, a faith that found a permanent home, it seems, in the U.S. But the Underground Man continues to survive as well, defying that faith, thumbing his nose at progress and prosperity, insisting on his own caprice if only to prove that the human soul is a not "simply an extraction of square roots." I met him one bitterly cold January in the Mall of America.

A friend of mine who works with an alliance of homeless persons in Minneapolis had given me his name (I'll call him "Tom") and told me I would find him working at the Rainforest Cafe. One of Steve Schussler's innovations at the Rainforest was an aggressive policy of employing the homeless; that is, actively recruiting them, maximizing their chances of successful employment, and paying them a good wage. When I asked Steve why he was making the effort he said, "I know what it's like to lose everything you have. When that happens to you it changes the way you look at the world."

Most of the homeless he hired were defeated by the requirements of regular employment: appropriate hygiene, showing up for work, staying off drugs. Tom was the only homeless person who had remained on the job for several months. He and Steve had become friends of sorts; after decades of uneasy courtesies from liberal do-gooders, Steve's no-bullshit frankness was a breath of fresh air. Tom had even done some work in Steve's home in St. Louis Park. One day Steve opened a drawer in his bedroom that contained a pile of unused wallets.

"Take one," he told Tom, who shook his head and declined.

"Steve," he said, "what am I going to do with a wallet?"
What he didn't tell Steve was that the reason he had no use
for a wallet was that he spent almost all his paycheck on
dope. He had been willing to meet reasonable expectations.
He came to work on time, he bathed more regularly than was
his custom, he even established a "permanent" residence. A
drug-free life, however, was not a reasonable expectation.

Drugs had been a part of Tom's life for as long as he
could remember, both buying and selling. "If you want to
use drugs," he told me, "you have to deal drugs." The list of
those he was familiar with was fairly exhaustive, old classics
and state-of-the-art innovations. He was not entirely comfortable with the requirements his need imposed on him. An
all-round handyman at the Rainforest, he would have preferred to work ten hours a day seven days a week, not for
the money but to control his consumption of chemicals.

We sat in his "office" (a desk, a chair, and a lot of inventory) behind the walls of Bloomingdale's on the Mall's second level and he told me about growing up in Minneapolis.
His mother had inherited money, he claimed, and his father,
who had no more than a sixth-grade education, earned more
than one hundred thousand dollars a year at National Cash
Register. They had a big house and Tom and his brothers
each had his own bedroom. Not a drinker himself, the father
nevertheless stocked a full bar in the home. "If you wanted
to drink all you had to do was go downstairs." So the boys
drank. They got into trouble at school, committed petty
crimes, got sent to reform school. One of the brothers committed suicide when he was twenty-one. But his folks were

wonderful parents, Tom insisted. His childhood could not have been happier.

So happy, in fact, that Tom ran away and joined a carnival called "Heart of America," a network of shows run by one family. He explained to me several carnival scams—the "alibi agent with a semi-flatie," the cork gun, the hoop game. One night he came upon some of the ride boys raping a girl and he got into a knife fight, cut a guy bad. He had to leave "Heart of America," but he found a job with "Crouch and Son."

He was on the road, living "the life," and that meant occasional prison time. He did his share, state and federal. He didn't mind. "Kinda nice, really." If anything, it was easier to feed his drug habit there and he never had any serious conflicts. "I'm socially acceptable. I get along with everybody." There were millionaires in prison who ran drug businesses from their cells and one of them, recognizing Tom's potential, later set him up with clothing stores in Minneapolis and Chicago, leather and heroin boutiques. He was one of the middle men—"I was third in from the border"—but a very prosperous middle man. He had two apartments, two "old ladies," a Harley, and five cars. He carried a derringer in the pocket of his Brooks Brothers suit. He spent most of his money, though, on his habit. "I was so fucked up, I thought I was straight." The Mafia moved in and put an end to all that.

He headed down to Texas for another cycle of boom and bust. He worked his way up the West Coast to Portland, and there he found something that "turned my life around. Made life worth living." He had been a homeless person for some time, but one night under a bridge God spoke to him and said, "To live in this camp you have to do something positive for yourself." He understood what God meant. He had to do something positive for others and in that way do something positive for himself. He took responsibility. Working with churches, he mediated programs to feed the homeless.

He organized a community. "Camp Hope" he called it. "I was the Camp Hope head organizer, administrator, enforcer, mother, brother." Law and order required some violence. Once when he came upon thugs beating up an old man he threw gasoline on them and threatened to strike a match. Instead he leveled them with a pipe. "You had to be invincible to survive." Working with others, he carved out a small village with gravel paths, lumber, tarps, tents, couches, a barrel stove. "I wish I had pictures." And then the city of Portland came in with bulldozers. Camp Hope was in violation of any number of ordinances, to say nothing of due process. The whole enterprise was an embarrassing eyesore to taxpayers. Tom didn't give up without a fight, so eventually designated parties (herein to be unnamed) made him an offer he couldn't refuse: leave the state or go to jail.

Now he was back in the Twin Cities, doing odd jobs for the Rainforest Cafe in the Mall of America. One afternoon as we stood outside Bloomingdale's, he conveyed his utter indifference to the material glory around us with a terse remark and a pointed gesture. He had known real glory once in Portland. Back in Minneapolis, the place of his "roots," he was, more than ever, a rootless soul. He didn't consider the $250-a-month studio he shared with another addict "home." He didn't want a home. "Homeless people aren't necessarily poor," he told me. "Some of us just don't want to conform. I can live with or without money." By his own account his life had been a struggle to overcome the disadvantages of wealth. He was at peace with his contradictions—a born-again Christian with a drug addiction, an advocate for the homeless who fed them bread, hope, and heroin. He was a smart man who consistently made what even he conceded were stupid decisions. And knowing that, he wouldn't change a thing.

When Steve Schussler opened a Rainforest Cafe in Chicago, Tom went along to serve as a liaison to the homeless because Steve wanted to extend his policy of hiring the homeless with each new franchise. Several years later I dropped by the Mall's Rainforest Cafe to ask how Tom was doing. I learned that shortly after he went to Chicago he "disappeared." I also learned that there were no longer homeless employed at the Rainforest, though it was not clear if this was due to a change of policy.

I have to admit this news was not a surprise. A man who says that he can live without money and means it will not likely make a serious commitment to free market enterprise. So he's back underground, out of sight and out of mind. He's beyond the reach of well-meaning entrepreneurs, beyond the reach of any redemptive program a team of bureaucratic visionaries is likely to dream up. He doesn't need to be saved; he's been saved. He has accepted the Lord and they have worked out an understanding of unmerited grace that eludes even Lutheran comprehension. He knows all about methadone and twelve steps and incentives—been there, done that, a dozen times—and frankly, my dear, he doesn't give a damn.

He's standing in the shadows, flipping the bird at our relentless optimism, mocking our Mall just as Dostoevsky's Underground Man mocked the Crystal Palace.

> Now I ask you: What can you expect from man since he is a creature endowed with such strange qualities? Shower upon him every earthly blessing, drown him in bliss so that nothing but bubbles would dance on the surface of his bliss, as on a sea; give him such economic prosperity that he would have nothing else to do but sleep, eat cakes and busy himself with ensuring the continuation of world history and even then man, out of sheer ingratitude, sheer libel, would play you some loathsome trick. He would even risk his cakes and would deliberately desire the most fatal rubbish, the most uneconomical absurdity, simply to introduce into all this rationality his fatal fantastic elements.

Chapter Eleven

The Unknown God of the Mall

IN LATE SUMMER OF 1992, two weeks after the Mall of America opened, a Sunday service was organized by the Wooddale Church of nearby Eden Prairie. Six thousand worshippers thronged all four levels around the rotunda between Bloomingdale's and Sears and sang, "All hail the power of Jesus' name! Let angels prostrate fall," then listened to Reverend Leith Anderson's sermon, "The Unknown God of the Mall." Afterward everyone fanned out into the shops and the Camp Snoopy rides.

I myself was not there. I learned about the service the next day when I read about it in the papers and was struck by the title of that sermon: "The Unknown God of the Mall." I was immediately reminded of a common characterization of malls—cathedrals of consumption. The point of that phrase, I suppose, is that hedonistic materialism is the real religion of Americans. Religion, that is, in Paul Tillich's definition:

one's ultimate concern. I doubted that that had been Pastor Anderson's message.

Perhaps he used the Mall as a spiritual metaphor. I've listened to some fairly farfetched homiletic analogies in my time. God's naval fleet: fellow-ship, steward-ship, etc. The trinity viewed as a three-ring circus in a sermon titled "Under God's Big Top." (I'm not making this up.) Many people love it when a priest or minister brings the Gospel down to earth, connecting pop culture with the Creator. Robert Short's *The Gospel According to Peanuts* was the top nonfiction best seller in 1964 and eventually sold over ten million copies. In his introduction, Short quoted Tillich, Barth, Cassirer, J. D. Salinger, T. S. Eliot, Hamlet, and Kierkegaard, the latter two repeatedly. The chapter titles give a good idea of the book's emphasis: "The Whole Trouble," "Original Sin," "The Wages of Sin is 'Aaaughh!' " "Good Grief!" "The Hound of Heaven," and a "Concluding Unscientific Postscript." Apropos of Snoopy, Short observed, "When the great German philosopher Hegel scoffed at Schleiermacher's declaration that the core of religious faith was the feeling of *absolute dependence*, Hegel said that of all creatures, then, the most religious must be the dog. In this, Hegel was closer to the truth than he realized." Ten million copies sold.

Short went on to write two other books, *The Parable of Peanuts* (1968, with a chapter entitled "Jesus—the Dog God") and *Short Meditations on the Bible and Peanuts* (1990). He has lightened up a bit on Schulz's spiritual vision: "Tolstoy believed love is what it was all about, that people were capable of this, that the spirit of love was inherent in people. So

Tolstoy wanted to withdraw from culture, live simply, working with his own hands. I think Sparkie's religious orientation is typified by Tolstoy."

What would Sparkie Schulz make of a worship service in a shopping mall—indeed, in Camp Snoopy? For much of his life, he has been a devout Christian of a strenuously nonsectarian kind. He scrupulously avoids, on principle, any hint of political innuendo in his strip. Lucy would call him wishy-washy, but a more sympathetic assessment would speak of tolerance. The only thing Schulz cannot tolerate is intolerant dogmatism. He is also skeptical of wishy-washiness carried to an extreme.

"I am very fearful," he was quoted as saying in 1968, "of a church which equates itself with Americanism. This is a frightening trend: people who regard Christianity and Americanism as being virtually the same thing."

Was that what those folks from Wooddale Church were celebrating, Americanism? Jesus drove money-changers from the temple; would he also have driven worshippers from a shopping mall? Hard to say. He was fairly open-minded, but he knew a scam when he saw one.

The Unknown God of the Mall. I just couldn't let it go. I've always been interested in religion. Not just Christianity, but also Judaism, Taoism, Buddhism, Hinduism, Islam, animism. I've never been interested in fake religion, however—scientology, Americanism, California dreaming. Was this Unknown God of the Mall the genuine article?

I recalled those great ceremonies and rituals throughout the year when we gather in malls to celebrate what the experts call "retail drama." The biggie, of course, is Christmas, a festival that stretches over two months and accounts for forty percent of retail sales nationally. The Mall opened its first Christmas season with a grand parade in its rotunda. That space was dominated by Snoopy's dog house, newly constructed and thirty feet tall, it seemed; it was draped with huge Christmas lights and surrounded by oversized, gift-wrapped packages and fir trees laden with ornaments. The biggest tree of all had burst through the dog house roof, as if to say that nothing can set a limit to Snoopy's desires. In front of the house people drifted back and forth on the gleaming escalators that crisscrossed overhead; behind the house other forms floated up and down in shining carriages of glass. Past the escalators the multicolored lights of Camp Snoopy flashed through the trees, the spinning brilliance of the rides bursting like fireworks in an enchanted forest. The encircling balconies of the Mall's upper levels were thronged with spectators, angelic hosts haloed in the dazzling neon of the shops beyond, and beyond them, way up on the fourth level, the nightclub marquees. The hyperspace was charged with innumerable winking lights, a meteor shower in which Woodstock and his feathered friends hung suspended under bright parachutes. Popcorn incense filled the sanctuary. It was otherworldly.

In front of Snoopy's dog house, Santa dismounted from his float and was helped out of his robe, a mantle of rich, white fur flecked with dark gray. Flashbulbs popped and cameras rolled as he removed his red, white-trimmed cap and seated himself before Snoopy's door. He was Norman Rockwell's Santa, the Night Before Christmas Santa, white hair

248

and white beard, small reading glasses perched on his ruddy, merry face. Parents lifted children onto their shoulders so they could glimpse his radiance and know for certain he exists.

Two weeks later I was sitting on a bench in Camp Snoopy. Fourteen shopping days till Christmas. The Mall was packed; it was the season of Advent, the season of quiet reflection leading up to the celebration of Jesus's birth. Most of the shoppers seemed merry. Harried if not merry myself, I was resting, preparing to find my car and drive home. When I bent down to tie a shoelace, I noticed something tiny. It was an ant carrying a crumb as large as it was. Two miracles: (1) In all this hubbub, the crush of bodies and synesthesia, how did this insect register on my radar scanner? (2) How did he ever get in here? I watched him wander off.

That evening at home, I remembered an essay on ants by Lewis Thomas, a piece in his first book, *Lives of a Cell*. I pulled the book from the shelf and found the essay.

"When social animals are gathered together in groups," Thomas began, "they become qualitatively different creatures from what they were alone or in pairs." He went on to reflect upon locusts and termites. Then this sentence: "Bees and ants have no option when isolated, except to die." Gee. I thought about my Mall ant. What crazy Robinson Crusoe adventure had brought him into Camp Snoopy? Maybe he rode in on a shoe or a pant leg, like a virus hitching a ride on a 747. He was probably very resourceful, but even a Robinson Crusoe ant cannot live by bread alone. Perhaps he had already perished. Cause of death: being alone.

On the other hand, maybe he was a sign that there are other ants in the Mall, possibly a colony. Had they been there from the start, sneaking in as the foundation was laid? But how could any ant colony have survived that cataclysmic earthquake, a vast upheaval that went on for months and months? They couldn't have made it in *after* construction; it seems unlikely that a whole colony could navigate in on shoes and pants. And the Mall's artificial surfaces would prohibit burrowing or hill building. A colony might settle into the soil at the base of one of the many live trees in Camp Snoopy, but they would surely be noticed by one of the botanical caretakers that tend the Mall's expensive fauna.

I was pretty certain by now that my Mall ant was a goner, and I pondered the lessons of his fate. "The social insects," Thomas reflected, "especially ants, have been sources of all kinds of parables, giving lessons in industry, interdependencies, altruism, humility, frugality, patience. They have been employed to instruct us in the whole range of our institutional virtues, from the White House to your neighborhood savings bank."

I turned back to my shelves and searched for another book, one about Indian myths and symbols. I found what I was looking for, a story in one of the Upanishads about the god Indra. A great monster had imprisoned the waters of the earth and produced a terrible drought. Indra slew the monster and released the waters and restored the world to light. To celebrate his victory, he set his master builder to construct a magnificent palace. "But as the work progressed, his demands became ever more exacting and his unfolding visions vaster.

He required additional terraces and pavilions, more ponds, groves, and pleasure grounds. Whenever Indra arrived to appraise the work, he proposed new marvels to be contrived."

His master builder, in despair, exclaimed, "There is no end to his desire," and went to the divine Creator, Brahma, to appeal for help. Brahma took his appeal to Vishnu, the Supreme Being, for whom the Creator was but an agent.

One day a beautiful boy appeared at Indra's gate and asked for an audience with him. So extraordinary was the boy's loveliness that he was ushered in to the god.

"Welcome, young man," Indra said to him. "What brings you here?"

"I have been told," the boy replied, "that you are building such a palace as no Indra before you ever built."

"Indra before me," the god said, "—what are you talking about?"

"Indras before you," the boy answered. "I have seen them come and go, come and go. Vishnu sleeps in the cosmic ocean, and the lotus of the universe opens from his navel. On the lotus sits Brahma, the Creator. Brahma opens his eyes and a world comes into being, governed by an Indra. Brahma closes his eyes and a world goes out of being. When Brahma dies the lotus goes back and another lotus blossoms and another Brahma. Galaxies beyond galaxies in infinite space, each a lotus, with a Brahma within it, opening his eyes, closing his eyes. And Indras? There may be wise men in your court who could tell you the number of drops in the oceans of the world or the grains of sand on the beaches, but no one could count those Brahmin, much less those Indras."

While the boy spoke, an army of ants paraded across the floor. The boy laughed when he saw them, and his voice shook Indra's palace with a terrible thunder. Indra's hair stood on end; his throat went dry.

"Why do you laugh?" the proud being asked in a breaking voice.

The boy replied, "I laughed because of the ants. The reason is not to be told. Do not ask me to disclose it."

Unable to move, Indra regarded the boy before him.

"O wisdom incarnate," the king pleaded with a new and visible humility, "reveal to me this secret, this light that dispels the dark."

Only then did Vishnu open to the god his hidden wisdom. "O Indra, those ants, filing in long parade, each was once an Indra. Like you, each by virtue of pious deeds ascended to the rank of a king of gods. Now, through many rebirths, each has become again an ant. This army is an army of former Indras."

As you might expect, Vishnu's visit brought an end to Indra's extravagance. Filled with remorse, the king repented and learned to live with less. Even a god, it seems, must accept some limits on desire.

Several years later, again in the Mall in the season of Advent, I opened a glossy brochure and read:

Forget about cloning sheep in Scotland, Mall of America is on the verge of creating its own high-tech twin. What Epcot did for Disney World may be the only sizable comparison to the ambitious ideas being discussed for Phase II construction at Mall of America. One proposal for